M.A.D.
MONEY

Money After Divorce, Death or Disaster

"7 Commitments to Help You Get Your Entire
Money Life"

Kemberli M. Stephenson, MBA

M.A.D. Money – Money After Divorce, Death or Disaster

Copyright © 2016 Kemberli M. Stephenson

Published by: AXIS Financial Group, LLC *Publishing Division*

Printed in the United States of America

Editor: Ink Pen Diva Manuscript Critique Services, LLC

Book Cover & Interior Design: AXIS Financial Group, LLC *Publishing Division*

Stephenson, Kemberli M.
M.A.D. Money – Money After Divorce, Death or Disaster: 7 Commitments to Help You Get Your Entire Money Life.

ISBN-13 (eBook): 978-0-9983916-1-8
ISBN-13 (paperback): 978-0-9983916-0-1

Special discounts are available on bulk quantity purchases by book clubs, associations and special interest groups.

For details email: hello@kemberlistephenson.com
or call (919) 859-3456

For additional information, visit
www.KemberliStephenson.com

DEDICATION

To God

All the Glory, Honor & Praise belongs to You.

To my parents, Oscar Sr. & Elizabeth
Thank you for teaching me the value of education.

To my guys, my sons, Christopher & Tyler
Thank you for giving me a reason to smile.

To My "Rock", Jay
Thank you for being the shoulder on which I cry and stand.

ACKNOWLEDGEMENTS

I would like to take this opportunity to thank my supporters along my journey to publishing my first book. The road has been long, arduous and filled with detours, but I made it to the end with your help!

First, I'd like to thank Tamika Sims, Writing Coach Extraordinaire. You saw the potential in me and served as the midwife I desperately needed to birth this baby. Your firm yet loving guidance has made this journey easier to travel. Without your support and confidence, I could have never gotten this project off the ground.

To all my coaches, formal and informal, thank you for sharing your wisdom, tips and skills with me. Learning the inner workings of marketing, social media and publishing is a mountain I could not begin to climb without you.

Thank you to my sister, my friend, and voice of reason ~ Chauntele Holley. Thank you so very much for your love, support and pushing me when I needed it most.

To Adrienne & Melaniece, not only are you my sorority sisters, you are my true friends. Thank you for the talks, encouragement and fun over the years.

To my oldest friends, Sharon & Samantha, I could not have gotten this far without your lifelong friendship, prayers and unconditional love. Thank you.

To my parents, Pastor Oscar & Reverend Elizabeth Holland, thank you for being an example of real love.

To Kevin, Oscar II & Sharon, I am super proud to be your sister.

To The Leverett Clan, thank you for embracing me and loving me unconditionally.

To my extended family and friends, I thank you for loving me through this project and for not holding it against me when I couldn't attend a function, talk for hours on end, or otherwise be available because I was on a deadline.

To Sharole, I've loved watching you blossom into the woman you have become. Thank you for letting me hang out with you on the journey.

For teaching me how to love, laugh and trust again, you will forever be my biggest comfort, my brightest smile and my best friend. I love you Jay.

To my two biggest accomplishments and the other two musketeers in this trio, my world would be incomplete without you. Christopher & Tyler, the love I hold in my heart for each of you is incomprehensible. You have given me nothing but joy and are my reason for breathing. Nothing makes me more proud than being your mom. I love you both to infinity times infinity times infinity!

Table of Contents

INTRODUCTION

Change is an inevitable part of life. Each potential change brings about a decision on how to dill with the turning point. In the span of a lifetime, we will all face thousands of potential turning points. My hope is that this book will be one of those for you. I'm hopeful that through these pages, you are able to feel all the love and kindness I feel as I pen these words.

Whether you are an UNMarried woman because you are divorced, widowed, single or soon to be single, the insights and commitments you will learn about in this book will have a tremendous impact in your life. When you picked up *M.A.D. Money – 7 Commitments to Help You Get Your Entire Money Life*, you started on a journey to financial health, satisfaction, independence and abundance! You are well on your way to achieving the financial momentum you have longed for!

It's so important for me to share this thought with you as you begin this journey - 'You don't become financially independent looking at the outside alone. It takes more inner work than anything else to finally live the financially abundant lifestyle you so desire.' Having said that, you might be wondering if this is yet another book filled with only feel-good, emotionally charged or impractical advice. You might be asking yourself if this a book that focuses on material gain as a success barometer. The answer is NO!

This book is as practical as much as it is spiritual. Don't worry....I don't mean spiritual in a religious rules based sense. I mean spiritual as in a connection with your inner spirit and your guiding light that is sure to help you along your journey to achieve solid financial footing.

Perhaps you've been challenged with meeting your financial obligations as a single mother. Maybe you're a widow facing life alone after your spouse died, or you may be a divorced woman looking to get back on your feet after your marriage has ended. Regardless of why you are or how you became UNmarried, *M.A.D. Money* will help you heal your financial wounds, holistically create a new money mindset, and propel you into a more secure financial future!

CHAPTER ONE

COMMIT TO ACCEPTING YOUR REALITY

Chapter 1

Commit to Accepting Your Reality

As I sat down in the chair, the knot in my stomach rose up to my chest. As I began to speak, my voice cracked. My emotions were doing it again. They were betraying me. They were telling the truth when I wanted to cover it up. They were stopping me from sharing the story as I'd told it for the past 4 years. My tears wouldn't allow me to simply say "I'm ok." or "It's all good." Not this time. Not to this woman.

I'm not sure if it was because of how she looked at me with the half smile – half smirk that said she got it. Maybe it was the way she leaned back in her chair with her legs crossed and her hands in her lap. I don't know if it had something to do with her tight auburn dreadlocks reminding me of Mother Earth's all-natural, unadulterated, authentic beauty. Whatever it was, I felt compelled to be absolutely honest and I felt safe doing it.

In that moment, I knew it was ok for me to let my guard completely down. There was nothing I could say to shock this woman or make her feel anything but love and compassion towards me.

Gerri was my savior. She was my teacher. She was my therapist; my sister; my confidante; and my friend. Her wisdom was both a pumice stone and a sharpening rod. When I was with her, I couldn't lie – not even to myself. She wouldn't allow it. She always kept it real with me. She didn't allow me to sugar coat my situation. I had to tell the truth.

The truth was I was scared. I felt hopeless. I couldn't understand how my life, my future that had once held so much promise, had come to this place. For four years, I pretended I was fine. I covered up my feelings, my fears and my financial truth from everyone – including myself. Gerri helped me come out of hiding and face reality.

If I had to have a single goal for this book, it would be that it would help you do the same. My wish is that *M.A.D. Money* will help you uncover your money truths so you can deal with them head on. I want you take you on a journey of financial recovery and restoration.

Fantasy Island

During the 1980's, there was a popular television show called Fantasy Island. I loved this show. During each weekly episode, the characters would leave their regular lives and travel to a remote island where all of their fantasies would come true during their visit. The island staff would ensure that whatever the dream was, the guest would be able to experience exactly what he or she desired.

The problem was that each of the fantasies came with a hefty price tag. The price to be paid went beyond mere dollars and cents. It would likely include some dangerous, heart breaking or somehow unimaginable truth. Thanks to the magic of television, the characters would typically learn the lesson and come through the experience without much more than a scratch and they did it all within the one hour timeslot for the episode.

I unfortunately wasn't so lucky with my fantasy life. Unfortunately for me, my lesson took more than 22 years to fully grasp. From the time I married until 4 years after my divorce was finalized, I found myself deep in the pits of desperation and denial.

My dream was to have a perfect family life. To me that meant a family that by society's standards was whole. It meant a husband, a wife and at least 2 children living in a beautiful subdivision near great schools. It meant that money was never a problem and that there was always enough for annual family vacations, weekly dinners out, date nights, and AAU sports teams for the kids. These were all things I rarely saw growing up in Philadelphia. Money was always tight even though my mom worked 3 jobs to support us at times.

Until I was nine, I was raised by a single mother. My biological father was absent from my life. I didn't want that lifestyle for my sons. I desperately wanted them to grow up in a two parent household. I would do or surrender to just about anything to keep my family together. Because of my deep desire to make my marriage work despite its challenges, my ex-husband had found my weak spot. He realized that he could treat me terribly and I'd accept it for the sake of the children.

I was living the classic life of an abused woman but because the abuse had rarely turned physical (it did happen twice), I convinced myself that my marriage was typical. I kept the verbal and emotional abuse a secret from my family and friends. I was isolated from those that loved me the most despite seeing them regularly. How could that be? The simple answer is when you allow people to believe that all is well in a marriage that's anything but, you've insulated your life from outside intervention and isolated yourself in a cell of your own making.

I made light of the complete control my ex-husband had over our finances. It didn't matter that I was the primary breadwinner in our household. I had no idea how much money we had from week to week. There were many days when I had to ask if there was enough in the account to buy gas to go to work or for lunch for the week. Despite the fact that I made almost 4 times the salary he did, he controlled the finances. He wrote the checks and spent the money the way he wanted to spend it. It wasn't until we were separated that I learned exactly what and who he was spending our money on.

For years I pretended the problem didn't exist. I ignored all the warning signs. I asked questions, but when the answers didn't make sense, I didn't push back hard or often enough. After 18 years, 2 kids, 7 relocations, multiple incidences of infidelity, restraining orders, abuse and both suicide and death threats, my marriage was irreparably over.

I can't help but think if I had not been so adamantly attached to living in the fantasy of a happy marriage with this person, I might have been able to save myself a boat-load of heartache and frustration.

I Was an Impostor

As a double degreed finance major, I spent over 20 years climbing the corporate ladder, running various businesses and trying to make my mark on the world. I had ascended the ranks to senior manager for some very large companies during my career. It was my job to know the numbers backwards and forwards and to be able to communicate any hiccups in the financials that could potentially cause the company to miss its projections. I was great at my job. I was so great at it, annual promotions and sizeable salary increases were commonplace for me.

At home, it was a different story however. I struggled to stay afloat when it came to my personal finances. After my divorce, I quickly ran through my savings and was living with the fallacy of making "good money." However, with a hefty mortgage, massive student loan debt, and two sons to get through college, my financial outlook was bleak. I couldn't tell anyone about it though.

When my divorce was finalized, I was overjoyed thinking I could finally move on with my life. I was free! I thought I would be able to put the past behind me and live the life and the lifestyle I had always dreamed about. What I didn't consider was that along with the house and primary custody of my sons, I walked away with 100% of the debt that had accumulated over the past 18 years.

My initial divorce decree did not include any provisions for child support and as such, I was awarded the total financial responsibility of paying for college for both kids. Many states legally stop child support when the child reaches 18 or graduates from high school. I lived in a state where this was the case. Unfortunately, my ex-husband used the law to his advantage and provided less than 2% of the total cost of tuition to either of my sons' education funds. It was up to me to make sure the boys had everything they needed for school.

Two years after my divorce, I finally pursued child support for my youngest son. Due to the state child support calculation formula, I received very little child support from my ex. My oldest son was 18 when the divorce was finalized and because my income was much higher than my ex-husband's was, I received very little support for my youngest son. There was no 50-50 rule in the state we lived in. At the time, I didn't think I cared. I thought my freedom was worth every penny I would have to pay on my own.

Emotions clouded my judgment. Thinking back on that time, I made the right choice by choosing divorce. However, along with good legal counsel, I should have also gotten good financial counsel. However, at the time, I thought I could make those decisions by myself simply because I had not one, but two finance degrees and had worked in corporate finance for my entire career. This could not have been further from the truth.

I was in so deep, if it weren't for my weekly pay schedule, my bills would have fallen behind much sooner than they did. In reality, I was way behind on my financial obligations, but I was floating my bills with ninja-like skills. I figured out exactly how many days I could let a bill go before utilities were disconnected or before a late payment would hit my credit report. As the months went by and carrying all of household expenses alone became more difficult, I moved further into the deep waters of debt.

The weight of the financial burden was heavy. The stress from keeping it all a secret from my family was even heavier. My health suffered. I put on weight. I rarely did anything outside of work and home. My mental health began to show the effects of living a lie. I finally sought the help I needed. Enter Gerri.

Gerri was a therapist who specialized in helping women get over divorce and abandonment issues. Boy, did she have her work cut out for her. Not only did she help me through various stages of divorce recovery, but as a by-product of that work, she helped me recognize and begin to fix my money issues.

Acceptance Doesn't Equal Agreement

The first thing Gerri and I worked on together was helping me devise a strategy to leave the fantasy world I'd created behind and to begin to accept and embrace the reality of my situation. Accepting the reality of your life is a powerful step towards getting your life back on track. It took a great deal of hard work, lots of tears and boxes and boxes of Kleenex to finally accept and stand in my truth, but it was all so worth it. And if I can do it, so can you.

The very first lesson Gerri taught me along the journey was that I didn't have to agree with my current situation in order to accept it and deal with it. In fact, because both my mindset and my finances were in such bad shape, the only acceptable thing to do was to totally and unequivocally separate myself from them and the havoc they were wreaking over my life. But first, I would have to face the situation head on.

Oftentimes, the truth is a big pill to swallow. Accepting reality is the most important step on the path to your financial comeback, but it's also the hardest. Part of the challenge of acceptance is understanding what it means to completely accept your reality and what that acceptance should look like.

Acceptance begins with being open to the possibility that there is a problem. Once we're open to the possibility that a change needs to happen, we can then fully acknowledge what that change could and should look like. The key is knowing that there will be work involved and no change happens overnight. You may face setbacks and fear on the journey, but with the proper tools and support system in place, you can overcome any setback that comes your way.

You Have to Accept It to Change It

To fully grasp and accept your reality goes beyond what you see on paper or in your bank balance. It's far bigger than the things that stare you square in the eyes. It also includes the emotions that come with those numbers and feelings that need to be left behind. The feelings I'm speaking of are blame, guilt, shame, resentment and regret. When you can combine the facts with the consequences, but release the negative feelings that knowing brings, you can say you've accepted reality and are in a good place.

So, as we dig deeper into the 7 Commitments, there are a few feelings that are not allowed on the journey. They won't fit into your luggage for the trip. So let's dump them right now, shall we? Say this with me:

No Blame – No Guilt – No Shame – No Resentment – No Regrets

Here's the thing – everything you've gone through to get to where you are today has been a necessary part of your journey through life. Everything. But now that you are here – now that you are ready to commit to healing your money issues – there are things that you no longer need on the journey. Their purpose has been fulfilled. You've experienced what was required and learned the lessons that they were meant to teach. It's time to let them go now. I find that mantras help me quite a bit when I'm working on changing my mindset. Say this mantra with me again and release those feelings from your spirit, lighten your luggage so we can move to the next stop on your journey to financial success.

"I release all feelings of blame, guilt, shame, resentment & regret from my life and in their place I embrace, happiness, ownership, strength and joy."

Accepting reality sets you free from the bondage of negative self-talk and sets you up for success. Accepting where you are brings the secret out of the closet and into the light of day so you are then free of your past mistakes. Once you accept the reality of your situation and release the negative emotions around it, you can then begin to live in the present and plan for the future.

Acceptance creates space in your life for choice. Having a choice is powerful. Having a choice is the difference between staying stuck and moving towards your financial goals. When we finally choose to accept our current reality as it is, we can then create an atmosphere of change in our financial situation.

Understanding and accepting my financial reality cleared the path for my journey to financial stability. Gerri and I didn't spend a lot of in-office sessions going through the nitty-gritty details of my finances, but she was quite fond of giving exercises as homework from our sessions to help me put what we discussed into practice. Homework exercises help to activate your newly developed knowledge and help to create better habits in your life.

Here's a bit of homework for you to help you begin to acknowledge, understand and accept your current financial situation. Only after you've taken these steps can you move into the other six commitments that will help get your financial life going and the money flowing in the right direction.

Step 1 – Get Organized

Pull copies of all financial and legal documents for example:

Bank Statements

Credit Card Statements

Utility Bills

Pay Stubs

Credit Reports

Divorce Decree

Tax Return

Insurance Policies

Child Support Agreements

Lease Documents

Other Financial Documents

Compile it all into a single document so you can understand it. This can be done electronically or manually. Keep it as simple as possible. Here's an easy way to manually create this part of the exercise:

On a single sheet of paper draw 4 evenly spaced lines from top to bottom. This will create 5 columns on your page.

Label the columns as follows: Name, Last Payment Date, Past Due Amount, Total Outstanding Balance, & Minimum Amount Due

Ex. 1

NAME	LAST PAYMENT DATE	PAST DUE AMOUNT	TOTAL OUTSTANDING BALANCE	MINIMUM AMOUNT DUE
		$	$	$
TOTAL		$	$	$

Go through your bills & fill in the columns

Add up the amounts in the Past Due Amount, Total Outstanding Balance and the Minimum Amount Due columns.

Circle the totals in red ink.

Step 2 – Acknowledge It

In front of a mirror, say the following sentence out loud as you are looking yourself in the eye (insert your own numbers into the blanks) "I currently owe a total amount of $_____ on my debt and bills." Close your eyes and take 3 deep breaths. Open your eyes and repeat the statement as many times as you need to in order to really get it.

Step 3 – Understand It

The fourth step in this process is designed to help you understand what it means to be where you are. This boils down to consequences. Consequences are tricky and can easily put you into a defensive mode which can lead to feeling some of the very emotions we discussed earlier all over again. During this step, I encourage you to remember and repeat the mantra we practiced earlier:

"I release all feelings of blame, guilt, shame, resentment & regret from my life and in their place I embrace, happiness, ownership, strength and joy."

Pull out 2 different colored highlighter pens. Highlight each bill that is past due in one color. It doesn't matter if it's past due by 10 days or 90 days or more. If it's past due, highlight it. Now look through the list and using the other pen, highlight any of your bills that have negatively

16

impacted your credit report or that are incurring late fees on a regular basis. Finally, starting with the highest minimum balance due, number your bills in descending order.

Once you've taken this step, you should have a pretty clear picture of the areas that need the most attention as you begin to make the practical moves to get you to your goals

Step 4 – Decide to Change It

Now that you've accepted and have a solid understanding of exactly where you are financially, it's time to make a decision. According to Peak Performance Guru Tony Robbins, *"Decision making is a force that shapes destiny."* The key with this particular decision is that in order for it to be truly effective and lasting, it takes an unwavering commitment not only to the expected result, but also an unwavering commitment to stick to the decision process to reach that result. Making a lasting financial change takes more than the desire to live life differently. It takes the determination to be consistent with each individual step in the process.

Ask yourself: Do you want to stay in this place or are you ready to move forward? Do you want to continue to be afraid of the unknown or are you ready to face your challenges head on? I hope the fact that you're still reading this is a signal that you are ready to make the decision to change your situation.

That decision to remain consistent is the hardest part of the process for many. It's what actually stops us from committing to the end result.

We can't get to the end because we can't see our way to it. There's a simple three step process to committing to your decisions:

Decision Commitment Strategy

Know where to focus. You can choose to focus on the good or the bad. You can focus on the important things or the minutia. You can focus on the simple or the complex. You can focus on the past or the present. For your financial journey to be a success, you must choose to focus on the positive steps you are taking. Don't sweat the small stuff. It's not important. Keep the plan simple and the hard stuff will take care of itself. And remember, the present is much more important than the past ever was.

Embrace the meaning. When you're committing to achieve a result, you're really committing the meaning that the result will bring you. If your financial goal is to be debt free, it's unlikely that you chose that goal just so you can say, "I'm debt free." You really committed to that goal because of the meaning that being debt free brings to your life.

Perhaps being debt free means you will have the freedom to go on vacations with your family which provides the relaxation and rejuvenation you crave. Maybe becoming debt free is all about minimizing the stress that comes with constantly having to avoid answering your phone because of the debt collectors that call you. Maybe becoming debt free will simply allow you to pursue your passion of starting a non-profit or opening a business that you've dreamed about.

Embrace the true meaning behind the result you expect to receive when you reach your goals. It will go a long way towards helping you stick to the commitment that you've made to yourself.

Know what to do. Here's where many people make mistakes when it comes to planning. It's human nature to desire a good outcome. We hope for the best. When we're developing our plans and expect to commit to the end, we can't neglect the challenges that we will inevitably face while trying to reach our goals. The best time to prepare for our challenges is before they become reality.

When making a decision to commit, we should certainly include the good things. That's why we're committing, but we can't forget about the bad things that may accompany the good. So, plan for those things as well. In business circles, this is called contingency planning. Here's how to do that: Think of the possible challenges that could pop up as you're working on your commitment. Write them down. Next to each possible challenge, define your plan of action should that challenge present itself. For good measure, list a few solutions to each challenge. This way, when and if you face any of the challenges you've written down, you've already done the hard work for figuring out what to do. You can simply do it and keep moving forward on your journey.

Let's provide an example:

If your goal is to commit to becoming debt free within the next year and as a part of your commitment to that end result, you decide that you will pay an extra $500 each month towards your credit card bills. You are

19

invited to a party and would love to have a new outfit. That can be a big temptation if before you committed to the end result you didn't have a contingency plan in place.

Thank goodness you have one though. You see, you included this type of scenario in your plan and you made the commitment to wear what you have in your closet until you've reached your goal and if you absolutely had to have a new outfit that you would save for it or work extra hours to get it. You also set your payments up on auto draft on the 5th of every month. This helps to ensure that you meet your $500 extra payment before you do anything else with your funds each month.

When you're committed to both the end result and the process it will take to get there, you have a far greater chance at meeting your goals.

Once you've accepted your current reality and made the decision to commit to both committing to changing it and to the meaning you'll receive when you do, you'll be ready to move on to the 2nd of the 7 Commitments – Commit to Ownership

CHAPTER TWO

COMMIT TO TAKING FINANCIAL RESPONSIBILITY

Chapter 2

Commit to Taking Responsibility for your Financial Well Being

I was in my thirties before I graduated college. I initially started when I around 18, but stopped going after my freshman year. I re-entered college after my discharge from the military and after having my children, so I was well into my twenties before I seriously pursued earning my degrees. Despite waiting as long as I did to try college again, I finished both my undergraduate and graduate degrees within a few years of each other. However, during the years while I was in school, money was very tight for my family.

When I was discharged from the Navy and got my first corporate job, I was making very little money. My early raises were small because when you start off in a low wage job and your increases are based on a percentage of your income, it's really tough to get ahead. Over and over again, I was told that because I didn't have a degree, I couldn't enter the coveted ranks of management. So, I did what I believed I needed to do and signed up for college courses at one of the easiest schools to get into – The University of Phoenix. The University of Phoenix is a for-profit institution that was well known in active duty and veteran military personnel circles. Not only was it a good choice because of its distance learning programs (you never knew when you'd be transferred or would have to relocate), the school made it super easy to get the loans necessary to pay for classes.

Because I was trying hard to survive financially, I made some really poor decisions. I had a family to provide for. Despite two incomes we were still under water at the end of each month. Little did I know that the decisions I was making would have a lasting impact on my financial future.

What did I do? I did what so many students who get trapped into higher education debt do. I used portions of my student loans to help supplement my normal living expenses. It was legal and easy to fall prey to the trap because the funds were readily available.

Four years after my divorce, I found myself plagued with tens of thousands of dollars in debt including additional interest and fees because of those student loans. As I shared in Chapter 1, I was awarded most of the marital property and custody of our children, but I was also awarded responsibility for all of the debt that had accumulated during my 18-year marriage.

Sure, that money went towards helping the entire family survive during some very lean times, but in the end, it was me and me alone who was burdened with paying those bills off. For many years after my divorce was finalized, I blamed my ex for all of it.

I blamed him for being able to walk away, virtually scot-free, from any debt, worry and any real responsibility either personally or financially for what had taken place during our marriage. It took a long time to stop blaming him for it all and to begin to take responsibility for my part in this financial debacle.

The Blame Game

Before I could truly get control of my financial destiny, I had to take full responsibility for what had gotten me to the place in which I found myself. In my grieving process for my marriage, I went through all kinds of emotions including anger, resentment, bitterness and blame.

I blamed my ex for any and everything. I blamed him for ruining my dream of having a 'til-death-do-us-part' marriage. I blamed him for being a 'bad husband.' I blamed him for my stress acne. I blamed him for being overweight. I blamed him for all of our money problems past and present.

I even went a step further. I blamed his upbringing for his lack of money prowess. I blamed him for being born in a different country because that was certainly the reason that we didn't agree on money. I even blamed him for not making enough money to support his family because as the man of the house, it was his responsibility to take complete care of us, right? Wrong!

It's easy to believe that blaming others for our circumstances will help to solve our problems or at least deflect them. We blame others to protect ourselves from hurt, shame, and the truth. If we were to take a good look at what blame does, we'd find that blame is a dangerous emotion. When we blame others, we are actually doing the very opposite of what we set out to do. Instead of building ourselves up and protecting us, blame causes us to lose. Instead of defending us, it defeats us. When we blame, we give our power away. Blame is a game we can't win.

Playing The Blame Game is like walking on a treadmill. No matter how fast you go, you still end up in the same place you started. I was ready to get off the treadmill, but first I needed to understand why I felt the need to play the game in the first place. This would be the only assurance I had that I could avoid getting back onto the treadmill again.

Why We Blame

I began to do tons of research and reflection on why we blame. Here's what I learned. There are 5 reasons why we find ourselves blaming others for our circumstances:

1. **It's a defense mechanism.** Placing blame on someone else allows us to preserve our own sense of self-esteem. We naturally want to protect ourselves from pain and conflict and blaming someone else for a situation allows us this protection if only for a short period of time. Blaming another person also helps us avoid dealing with our own flaws and failings. If we blame our ex-spouse or deceased partner, we can pretend that we didn't have anything to do with the problems that were created.

2. **We want to inflict pain.** We often blame another person in order to inflict pain. We find this especially true in cases of divorce. Because we're angry or bitter, we lash out at our former spouse because we believe they deserve to hurt as much as we're hurting.

3. **It's easier than taking responsibility.** Blaming another person is often easier to do than if we were to accept full responsibility in our circumstances. We don't want our friends, family or loved-ones to think less of us or be disappointed. On the same note, we want to disappoint ourselves least of all. So, we blame others for our shortcomings, poor choices, indecision, or bad judgment.

4. **It helps us justify our own behavior.** This again is a way of avoiding our own pain in a situation. Blaming someone else allows us to justify our own choices. For example, it was difficult for me to accept some of the things my ex-spouse did during our relationship and I often thought 'Who does that?' about some of his actions. It took a while, but I finally realized the question I was really asking was 'How could I have chosen this person to marry?' What I was really doing was trying to justify my own choices.

   In large part due to my therapy sessions, I was able to accept the choices I made in my life and forgive myself for the bad ones. During those sessions, I learned a beautiful lesson of self-compassion.

5. **We're afraid.** This was the biggest eye opener for me when it comes to why we blame. We blame when we're afraid of facing reality or accepting responsibility. We're afraid of the consequences that being brutally honest might bring. We're afraid of who and what we might lose if we tell the truth of it all. We

fear what people might think of us or worse yet, what we might realize about ourselves.

Taking responsibility for our part in our situation can be difficult, but is absolutely imperative to moving forward in life. Taking responsibility is the only way to grow and develop personally, professionally, and spiritually. Responsibility has a certain character that makes it easy to identify. The ability to stand in our own truth, good or bad, is probably the top marker. A close second is the ability to verbalize your part in the situation. Lastly, having the strength and courage to smile at yourself in the mirror knowing what you know now, rounds out the top three characteristics of responsibility.

It's liberating. Shame often follows blame. If you live in that place it becomes difficult to shake the two of them off. Taking ownership or responsibility frees you from the burden of blame and shame.

I finally realized that I had to stop blaming my ex for *my* situation. I could have made better decisions back then. I could have and should have protected my most valuable asset - me. I didn't. I don't beat myself up about the decisions I chose to make. I realize that I wasn't in the best financial mindset at the time and like Maya Angelou said, *"When you know better, you do better."* I know better now.

Taking responsibility or ownership for your situation does not mean accepting someone else's actions or inaction as your own. We each have a significant impact on this earth and we each have to accept our roles in what happens to us. There's a saying 'It takes two to tango,' and yes each individual involved in any situation plays some role in it and therefore owns a piece of it. The key is to identify your piece and deal with that for yourself. Don't blame or beat yourself up for the consequence. Simply acknowledge it, feel it, and learn from it.

Responsibility builds confidence and self-esteem. It's easier to look someone in the eye when you know that you've owned something. Whether it had a good or a not-so-good outcome, it's still easier to look another person in the eye with confidence when all the cards are on the table.

Blame is a distraction. It takes your attention away from the truth about your situation. Taking responsibility for your financial circumstances allows you to live in the present and let go of the past. It propels you toward your success and your true financial destiny.

Letting Go & Accepting Responsibility

You've heard it before. Learn from the past. Don't make the same mistake twice. Never forget. While each of these axioms rings true, we can never allow the past to hold us back. You cannot live in the past.

Accepting responsibility takes both brain and heart power. In order to take responsibility for our actions, we first think about and learn from the past. That's the brain power. Letting go requires heart power. The learning is the easy part. The letting go takes real courage. I'm confident you can do it though. With the right direction, you can conquer the heart piece.

There's a simple 7 step process to letting go of the past, taking responsibility and focusing on your future.

The 7 Steps of Letting Go:

1. **Recognize when it's time to let go.** There always comes a time to fold. The key is letting go early enough to minimize your losses. Take notice of the signs. Feel confident that the signs are leading you in the right direction.

2. **Acknowledge the emotions that come with releasing the past.** Allow yourself to feel them. Don't ignore or push the feelings down. Let them come up so you can get them out.

3. **Give up the anger or resentment.** There's no need for anger. Here's the thing, everything happens for a reason. Each and everything that happens to us serves a purpose in our destiny. There's no need to be angry with the circumstances that play a role in our destiny. Without those circumstances, we would never become who we're created to become.

4. **Give up guilt and shame.** Remember that shame follows closely behind blame. There is no guilt or shame in living life and making mistakes. Let it go. Guilt and shame serve no purpose for you.

5. **Forgive.** Forgiveness allows you to move forward. Forgiveness buys you grace. Forgiveness releases negative energy and makes room for better things to happen for you. Forgive yourself for your mistakes and poor choices. Forgive your ex for his mistakes. Regardless of whether you have a direct conversation with him or

not, forgive him so you can move forward into your financial destiny.

6. **Reframe Your Focus.** Oftentimes we frame the circumstances surrounding divorce, death, or disaster from a negative perspective. While none of these situations are pleasant to experience, it's important that we view the circumstances that led up to the event in a way that helps us as opposed to hurting or holding us hostage to the event itself. If you're having difficulty letting go of the past, try reframing your focus.

7. **Live In the Present & Prepare for the Future.** You can't change the past. It's gone. As you begin to let go, you might wonder where you should focus your attention. It's extremely important to enjoy this time in your life. Live out loud. Make happy memories. And as you're embracing the day, prepare for a better, brighter future.

Change Your Perspective

As you make your way through the seven steps outlined above, expect to feel some internal uneasiness. Having a negative perspective about your past and your financial health is not unusual. However, it's important that you begin to reframe your thoughts. What is framing? Framing is how we mentally structure these areas. Framing gives meaning to our circumstances and is largely based on beliefs to which we ascribe.

I advise my clients to incorporate journaling, prayer and meditation to help you move through this process. Journaling is a cathartic practice that helps you get out of your head and helps connect you to some of your deepest feelings.

Below is a journaling exercise you can use to help you with the final two steps of letting go. As you take this important step towards reaching your financial goals, ask yourself the following questions:

> ➤ What are my personal priorities?

> ➤ What are my financial priorities?

> ➤ How do my personal and financial priorities align with my current lifestyle?

> ➤ What resources might I need to help me reach my goals?

> ➤ Am I taking the necessary steps to reach my goals?

> ➤ Have my past decisions helped me move towards my goals?

> ➤ What is the optimal decision I can make about my finances today?

> ➤ What do I believe about money?

> ➤ Why do I feel this way about money?

> ➤ If I have a negative perception of money, what can I do to change it?

> ➤ How will I feel when I reach my goal?

> ➤ Who can I ask for help to reach my goals?

> ➤ What might the consequences be if I don't focus on my priorities?

> ➤ Are my goals good for me? Do they serve me well?

> ➤ Do my goals serve those people who are important to me?

> ➤ How have my past experiences challenged me?

> ➤ How have my past experiences served me?

> ➤ What can I learn from my past?

> ➤ How might I use my experience to help someone else?

I encourage you to be compassionate with yourself as you go through this process. Motivate yourself or find a friend or circle of friends to help you traverse this unfamiliar terrain. Use daily affirmations, prayer, meditation and positive self-talk to help you face it head on and overcome it.

Don't be a slave to your past. Let go of the past to the degree that it no longer serves you. Reframe your focus. Live in the present and prepare for the future. Only through accepting responsibility for your current and future financial health can you begin to walk down the path to your financial destiny.

CHAPTER THREE

COMMIT TO GETTING SAGE ADVICE

Chapter 3

Commit to Getting Sage Advice

sage

/sāj/ *noun*

Wise through reflection & experience   2. Characterized by wisdom and good judgment.

Western Union

During the nineties, I received a desperate phone call from a friend's daughter who needed my help. She needed something from me that required a huge leap of faith on my part. She was hysterical. When she called, I could barely make out what she was trying to say to me over the phone.

The request required me to put myself and my family on the line, go against the wishes of some of my closest acquaintances, and set aside some of the plans that I'd made for me. I felt stuck between a proverbial rock and a hard place. After thinking about it for a day or so, I called her back and told her I would do what I could to help her.

She needed to live with me for a while. We initially didn't know how long that would be. She had a few personal items and some clothes, but everything she owned fit into a single suitcase. Once I agreed to allow her to stay, I put on my super-shero cape and jumped into action. I called the correct authorities to ensure we had the proper documentation for her to live with me. I called friends and borrowed a bed, winter clothes, and arranged for her to start school. I moved my two sons into a room together so she could have her own space. We made travel arrangements and she moved in.

It took three weeks for the honeymoon period to wear off. Quickly, the initial shock and gravity of her situation wore off and she began exhibiting the same behaviors that caused her to find herself in that situation in the first place. She was often disrespectful. She was emotional, scared and insecure. She was also a typical boy-crazy teenager. She disobeyed me on numerous occasions.

One day, while speaking with a friend's aunt, I told her about my situation. I shared the graphic details of how she came to stay with us. I explained that it was not only an emotional roller coaster, but also how it had become a financial hardship. I shared the stories about the major blowups with her and the times she lived under my roof and chose not to speak to me. We talked about how some of her family members said vile and ugly things to me. I told her how through it all, I felt as if I was being used.

The close acquaintances I mentioned earlier turned their backs on us because we didn't handle the situation the way they wanted us to. They thought we should have let her stay in the city where she'd been dumped and learn to fend for herself. I wanted to help her though. I knew she didn't know that place well enough to survive and I knew that she had the potential to do something with herself if she just had enough support. Because I went against their wishes, when times got tough, they refused to help and said things like, "I told you so." Yet, "I told you so," didn't help. So I turned to the counsel of my friend's aunt.

Her words to me were, "Oh, I wish you would have asked me about this before you brought her into your home. I would have told you to go to Western Union and just send money."

That conversation happened more than fifteen years ago and I remember it as if it was yesterday. Great advice has a way of sticking with us. These days, before I make any major decision, I seek wise counsel. Asking for advice from a trusted source is not a sign of weakness. It takes courage to ask for help, and it's the smart thing to do when you are unsure of your next move.

Wise Counsel

In this chapter, I want to help you understand how to choose the right adviser for your situation. I can't tell you how many women I've met at speaking engagements, church, and in my day to day travels who are paralyzed because they don't know where to start the process.

When it comes to getting control of your finances, there is an array of options. There are many different types of financial advisers and there are different *levels* of advice, but please be careful when making your selection. Anyone can call themselves a 'financial adviser.' However, there is a difference between giving general financial advice and providing financial services as a business.

Finding the right professional financial adviser is the key. My suggestion is to focus on three things when choosing someone to counsel you about money: Experience, Trust, & Compatibility. While there are many questions you must ask to help you make the right selection, the very first question that you must have a definitive answer to is:

"What results am I seeking as a result of working with this individual?"

Below I explain some of the differences between financial advisers and how you can make the best choice for your situation:

Certified Financial Planner™ *(CFP*®*)* – A Certified Financial Planner™ is an individual who has pursued rigorous financial courses and who passed the examination and experience tests to earn this designation. The CFP® examination is a test administered by the national governing board of Certified Financial Planners. After passing the rigorous exam, the candidate must then acquire up to 6,000 hours of work experience in the field before being awarded the final designation. A CFP® is someone who will help you in the areas of investments, insurance needs, estate planning and retirement planning.

Financial Planner – A Financial Planner aids individuals and corporations in planning their long-term financial objectives. A Financial Planner can offer many of the same services as a CFP®, but has not earned the right to use the designation by completing the requirements of the Certified Financial Planner Board of Standards, Inc., the body that oversees the CFP® designation. A Financial Planner will discuss your current financial circumstances, short and long term goals with you and recommend a financial program to help you achieve those goals.

Series 6 Licensee – An individual who holds a Series 6 license is entitled to register with the Financial Industry Regulatory Authority (FINRA) as a limited representative. This license holder is able to offer a limited array of services including mutual funds, insurance policies and variable annuities. This individual cannot sell corporate or municipal securities.

Series 7 Licensee – An individual who holds a Series 7 license that has passed the examination given by the Financial Industry Regulatory Authority (FINRA). The license is a general securities license and allows the holder to become an entry level stock broker. The licensee is competent, by FINRA standards, to trade securities, mutual funds, municipal series, stock options and variable contracts. Many license holders can be found working at brokerage firms.

Series 63 Licensee – It's important to note that states also regulate Financial Advisers. The Series 63 entitles the holder to offer securities in a particular state. The Series 63 is required of both Series 6 & 7 holders before they can sell securities. This license focuses on areas of ethics and fiduciary responsibility.

Certified Public Accountant (CPA) - Certified Public Accountant has passed the Uniform CPA exam given in the United States and has enough college coursework to earn a Master's Degree. Her focus area might include working for large corporations, government entities or providing tax and general accounting services. For individuals it's important that she provides tax planning, tax representation before the Internal Revenue Service and tax preparation & consulting services.

Financial/Money Coach – A Financial or Money Coach may hold any or none of the licenses or professional credentials listed above. The role of the Money Coach is focused more on behavioral and transformational practices rather than advising clients how to invest or plan their estates. A Money Coach combines sound coaching and psychological principals with practical financial strategies to help her clients transform their relationship to money.

What to Expect

When deciding to work with a financial adviser, there are a few things to consider. At the top of the list are professionalism and results. Other areas to be mindful of are fee structure, responsiveness, and philosophy.

Professionalism

The following list of questions will help you gauge an adviser's level of professionalism:

1. Have you been or are you currently involved in a lawsuit as a result of your advice?
2. What credentials do you hold?
3. How long have you practiced in this industry?
4. What types of structured programs do you recommend?
5. What professional associations or organizations are you affiliated with?

6. Which state(s) are you licensed in?

7. What is your level of professional education in this area?

8. What types of clients do you work with?

9. Do you accept fiduciary responsibility?

10. How often will you evaluate my situation and update your recommendations?

11. Do you think you're the best adviser for me and why?

Results

The following list of questions will help you better understand the results your adviser can deliver:

1. What references/testimonials do you have?

2. What results can I expect from working with you?

3. What do you expect from me as a client?

4. What size portfolios do you manage?

5. What specific services do you perform?

6. Will I receive regular updates of my financial accounts?

7. What systems do you recommend to help me with my financial situation?

8. How do you gauge success as it applies to working with clients?

9. What types of individuals do you work with?

10. How are your services different from other providers?

Responsiveness

Ask some of the following questions to help determine the adviser's responsiveness:

1. What are your office hours?
2. Do you have a website where I can learn more?
3. What is your turn-around time for inquires and problem resolution?
4. How are appointments handled?
5. Can I call you outside of a regularly scheduled appointment for quick questions?
6. Do you have administrative staff to help manage clients?

Fee Structure:

An adviser's payment and fee structure is a critical component in the decision to work with her. Be sure to find out the following:

1. How much do you charge?
2. Do you offer different levels of service?
3. What is your fee structure?
4. Did the person who referred me to you receive a fee for the referral?
5. Are your fees fully disclosed up front?
6. For Coaches – Do you offer refunds on any of your programs or services?

Philosophy

It's important that you and your financial adviser are compatible. Be sure to ask questions that will make you comfortable working with her:

1. What investment firms do you work with?
2. Are there securities that you adamantly advise against investing in?
3. How do you work with different risk tolerance levels?
4. Should I maintain a separate investment portfolio from my spouse?
5. Will you ensure that I fully understand your recommendations before moving forward?
6. For Coaches: How long does a typical relationship with a coach last?
7. For Coaches: How is coaching different from therapy or financial consulting?

How to Know Which Type of Adviser You Need

Before you can effectively choose the best adviser to work with, you must know which type of adviser is best suited for your circumstance. Let me share a few scenarios and make recommendations for the type of financial adviser to seek out:

Example #1:

You are facing divorce after 14 years of marriage. You have 2 children, a house, a couple of vehicles and vacation property. You have a sizeable retirement portfolio that is shared between you and your spouse.

You want to ensure that you exit the marriage with a fair share of the financial portfolio and want to minimize tax effects of dividing the assets.

You Need: A Certified Financial Planner & a Certified Public Accountant

Example #2:

You're a single parent of 2 children. You work full-time as a marketing director. You own your home, but you're deep in credit card debt. You feel like you're drowning under the weight of your financial obligations. You make a good salary and receive child support from your children's dad. You should have more than enough money to make ends meet, but for some reason there's always more month left than there is money in the bank to make it until the end. You want to start saving for the kids' college, but you can't seem to get your financial situation under control.

You Need: A Money Coach

Example #3:

You're a young widow with a 3 year old daughter. You've lived with your elderly parents since your husband died in a traffic accident. They help you with babysitting during your work hours and you help with household expenses. The insurance payout from the accident only covered the funeral expenses and a year's income. There's not much left You want to start saving for your daughter's education and provide for her in the event something were to happen to you. You dream of buying a home in a better neighborhood with better schools for your daughter. You would also like to start investing and saving towards retirement.

You Need: A Series 6 & 63 License Holder & a CFP®

How to Find the Best Adviser for Your Situation

When you begin your search and after you've determined the type of adviser you need, the next step is to ask around for referrals. The easiest place to start is by asking trusted friends and family members for their recommendations. Be sure to ask someone whose past or current financial circumstances are similar to your own. Advisers tend to build their client base with very similar clients.

Before you call an adviser or coach to make an appointment, visit their website and look up any available reviews. Do your own research and create a short list of names from the referrals you receive.

A great resource to find Financial Planners is the National Association of Personal Financial Advisers. The only advisers that our site recommends are fee-based advisers. This means the adviser does not earn a commission on specific investments they might recommend to you. This serves you because it allows the adviser to make recommendations based on client needs as opposed to potential earnings for herself.

The next thing you'll want to do is to visit the Financial Industry Regulatory Authority's website. Here you can research advisers that hold the CFP® designation and verify they are compliant with all requirements.

To vet a CPA, visit the American Institute of Certified Public Accountants for detailed information on how long a licensee has been certified. Each state also keeps records of licensees admitted to practice in the state. There is also a State Board of CPA's in every state. This is the body that regulates licensees. You can verify whether a CPA's license is current, if she has been at risk of having her license revoked and what firm she's affiliated with.

Money Coaches aren't as stringently regulated as other financial advisers. She might be a member of a coaching association similar to the International Coaching Federation (ICF™), but it isn't a strict requirement. However, it's a good idea to ask for references from a coach you want to work with. Be sure to check the references for yourself.

When it comes to reaching your financial goals and taking control of your financial destiny, you're the director and executive producer of your money story. It's your responsibility to pick the players for your team, and now you're equipped to make the best selections to ensure your money story has a very happy ending.

CHAPTER FOUR

COMMIT TO PROACTIVE PLANNING

Chapter 4

Commit to Proactive Planning

Mexico or Bust

I n early 2015, I was catching up with two friends on a three-way call. I've been friends with Sharon and Samantha since ninth grade and we've gone through life's greatest blessings and challenges together. From playing on high school sports teams to weddings; through military service and the births of our children; even through a run in with campus police and through a major car accident that nearly took our lives, our friendship has remained strong. In January of that year, we decided that having experienced so many other things together, it was time to embark on a getaway trip – just the three of us.

We scheduled bi-weekly conference calls (complete with a conference call number and automated scheduling app) because we wanted to plan this trip the right way. Honestly, it was easier to use a conference call number than to try to figure out how to do a regular three way voice call. We each had assignments and tasks to complete before the next scheduled call. We live in different states and are all heading towards 50 years old. Each meeting had an agenda and action items. We were strict with deliverables and deadlines. Yes, we were planning divas!

To save money and keep it simple, we decided to take a quick 4-day cruise to Mexico. We used a planning app to keep us on track, so we wouldn't forget anything. We set a deadline for me to get my passport since I was the only one of us who didn't have one yet, and the girls checked in with me weekly to see if it had arrived in the mail. We pre-planned the shore excursions and the sleeping arrangements. We even did some contingency planning to cover things like bathroom time and security code phrases (just in case).

We planned our trip like professionals. We left no stone unturned and incorporated checklists, apps, and other tools to help us have the trip of a lifetime. We were proactive about it because this trip was important to us. We hadn't taken a trip, just the three of us, since we were seniors in high school. We wanted this trip to go off without a hitch. It did! Well, sort of.

In the end, only two of us actually went on the trip because Sam's trip to Africa conflicted with our travel schedule. We didn't realize this when we made our deposit. We're still trying to figure out how we missed this, but we were able to receive a credit for her portion of the trip. She was listed as our third person and the cruise line allowed us to transfer those funds to our on-board activity fund. When planning a trip like this, it's important to be aware of all the fine details and negotiate ways to ensure you get the most for your hard-earned dollars.

It rained the entire time we were on the ship. The saying goes, "You can never trust Mother Nature." The ship wasn't as luxurious as we expected it to be. We should have expected this because, despite the beautiful, glossy, marketing photos, the ship was over 20 years old!

Nevertheless, Sharon & I had a blast, drank like sailors (hey, we're both proud Navy veterans) and made the most out of our four rained out days at sea.

Why You Have to Plan

With the three of us living in different states, if we had waited until the week before our departure date to decide to go on our girlfriends' getaway, our trip would have probably never happened. At the very least, instead of experiencing the joyous time we had, we would have experienced chaos. Instead of having a Plan B when the torrential rain came, we might have been stuck in a hotel room hiding from the weather.

Similar to planning the trip of a lifetime, it's crucial to plan your financial life. In this chapter, I want to share three reasons why you must commit to proactively planning your finances down to the smallest detail. Now, I'm sure there are plenty of other reasons to proactively plan, but these are three of the reasons that surface most often in my coaching practice.

Reason #1: Proactive planning allows you to measure your success.

When you develop a solid financial plan, it helps keep you on sure footing and gives you a clear indication when you're veering off track of meeting your goals. A solid plan is the best measuring stick to tell you how you are doing. Sometimes it looks as if everything is going well in our lives, but it seems so only because what we're experiencing is what we have become accustomed to. We can become satisfied with the mediocre without ever knowing it. We fall into the trap of thinking we are doing well because we seem to be doing as well as or better than the neighbors next door. The truth is we are really all just struggling to survive.

You can become so accustomed to just getting by that you become complacent. You stop believing there's anything more to life than the one you are already living. You stop planning. When you become complacent and stop planning, you're more likely to accept your poor financial state regardless of how bad it really is. Complacency blinds us to the reality of our situation which in turn makes decision-making much more difficult.

It is easier to tell the difference between good times and bad times when you have a strong financial plan to use as a yardstick for your personal situation. How often do you compare your situation with that of a friend's or someone else you might know? There's danger in comparisons. When you compare your situation to someone else's, there's a real likelihood you are only seeing what they want you to see. You might be looking at an exterior façade and missing the crumbling foundation. You do not have the background knowledge or the insight that explains how your friend came to be in her situation. You don't have all the facts and you likely don't know the back-story.

It's a much better approach to focus on your own reality. Compare yourself today to the "you" of yesterday. Be your own measuring stick. Do so by revisiting the plan you've created for your own finances.

Reason #2: Proactive planning helps you grow your nest-egg and your net worth.

Have you ever wondered why savings accounts are called nest eggs? I recently learned the original meaning of nest egg was a real or artificial egg placed in a nest to encourage hens to lay eggs there. Can you imagine your money actually working *for* you? The financial definition of nest egg is an amount of money saved for a specific purpose. That purpose might be to purchase a home, pay for college or retirement. Without careful planning, saving for big ticket items or retirement is nearly impossible.

Proactive planning also helps increase your net worth, the financial difference between what you own and the amount of debt you have. Through careful planning and meticulous record keeping, you can pay down your debt while increasing your assets. Let's use an example. When purchasing a vehicle with all cash, you're in a much better position to negotiate the price down to your liking. When you're using credit and a small down payment, you have no leverage to negotiate the vehicle's price. Bottom line, plan for purchases of big ticket items far in advance.

There's a saying, "When you fail to plan, you plan to fail." This axiom holds true in all areas of life, especially financial planning.

Reason #3: Proactive planning protects you against the fear of the unknown.

A few years ago, I worked for a recruiting agency. We worked hard to place professionals into contract jobs and permanent roles. I can't begin to tell you how many of my clients would take the first job offered to them, even if they knew it wasn't the right job just because they desperately needed the money. They were acting out of fear. Their biggest fear was not having enough money to make ends meet or to be able to survive. During numerous counseling sessions, I asked the questions about the ideal position they were hoping to get. You can always tell the candidates who had some savings from those who didn't because those were the ones who would hold out for the position that offered the advancement or the salary they were looking for.

Those that didn't have a financial cushion were often forced to accept a position that paid a lot less than their value and as such found themselves stuck in a catch-22 situation. Once they accepted the position, it became harder to find or make the time to search for a better job. They found themselves stuck. Remember, the power of proactive planning allows you to wait for the right opportunity to present itself and be prepared to deal with the unknown.

What to Include in Your Plan

As we prepared for our cruise to Mexico, I ran across an article online that included a "What to Pack for a Cruise' list. Along with the typical items you'd expect to take on vacation, the list included items many people neglect to pack for a Mexican cruise. Some of the things included on the "Don't Forget" list were extra hangers, a power strip, disinfectant wipes, a lanyard and a reusable water bottle. Who knew? Certainly not this cruise virgin! Think of this next section as your packing list.

The following is a short list of important components to a successful financial plan. This list goes beyond the standard and suggests some fun things as well.

Goals - You've probably heard the old adage, "A goal without a date attached, is but a dream." We're going to attach milestones a little later. For now I want you to dream. Think of all the things you've wanted to do, experience and feel in your lifetime. Financial goals shouldn't only include material items. The goals we're talking about here should also include feelings you want to have. Sometimes a certain level of financial independence can evoke pretty strong emotions. Perhaps it's taking that trip to Bali you've dreamed about, helping your favorite charity or going back to school. Reaching your goals brings feelings of accomplishment, happiness, fun and freedom.

When you're going through this exercise, have some fun with it. Get quiet and prepare your favorite drink and journal about the thoughts and emotions that until now have only lived in your sleep space. It's great to dream, but for this one I want you to dream out loud and in color. Dream big!

Your Why – Your why is one of the most important components of your financial plan. It is the foundation for everything else. Your why is the motivation for doing what it is you set out to do. Your why might be intrinsic or extrinsic. There's no right or wrong when it comes to your why. It's yours and nobody can define it better than you.

Whether your why is to create a legacy for your children or if it's to provide the financially independent lifestyle you've dreamed about since you were six, it's important to identify what it is and what role it plays in your financial plan. Once you identify your why, you can activate it as the motivational force you need to push you when you're feeling like you want to give up or to change the plan.

Your Now – It's very important to fully understand and accept your 'now'. We talked about this in detail in Chapter 1. Be sure to read that chapter if you happened to skip ahead. Your 'now' is your starting position. It defines your current financial position and tells you how much work you have to do to reach your goals. It also gives you a better idea of which method to pursue to achieve them. Your position should be clearly defined.

Your How – The 'how' in your financial plan is the methodology you will use to achieve your goals. It should include dates, amounts, strategies and a written execution plan. Are you using your 401k or an IRA to save for retirement? How much will you save every month? Who will you seek for financial advice when you need it? What percentage of your income will you put away for a rainy day? These are all questions you need to know the answers to.

Budget – This goes without saying. Having and using a budget is imperative as you strive to reach your financial goals. I have used a strict budget for the past eight years and it's been my saving grace on more than one occasion.

Did you cringe when you read the word 'strict?' While sticking to my budget is something I'm very strict about, I also include line items for fun, entertainment and personal development. So *strict* doesn't mean that you live like a pauper or never have any fun. Strict simply means planning for everything!

Savings Plan – A savings plan is simply the amount you plan to save daily, weekly, monthly and yearly. I advise my clients to start with an annual figure and break it down by the month, the week, and the day to determine if it's a realistic number. If your goal is to save $10,000 a year, but you can't seem to find the $1,000 a month to make that happen, it's time to revisit your annual savings goal.

Risk Plan – Early in 2014, a friend's mother passed. She had a small insurance policy through her employer but she didn't have a personal policy. Her children were unaware of the policy's existence and struggled to pull together the finances necessary to cover her funeral expenses. Since they didn't know about the policy, they did not reach out to their mother's employer to get the contact information for the insurance company. The employer didn't proactively reach out to the family with the information either. Seven weeks after the funeral, the siblings received an unexpected check from the insurance company. The additional stress they encountered while making funeral arrangements and during the weeks following their mother's burial, could have been avoided if only she had informed someone in her family of the policy's existence.

A risk plan is a fancy way of saying insurance. Insurance protects your loved ones and yourself in the case of a catastrophe or death. Be sure your financial plan includes copies of your insurance policies. This includes your homeowner's, life, auto, long-term care, medical and disability policies. Also be sure that someone whom you trust knows what you have, where your documents are stored, and how to access them when the time comes.

Credit/Debt Strategy – That's right. You should have a clearly defined credit/debt strategy. While retail credit cards can be dangerous, I realize that most people have at least one in their wallet. The key to managing your credit properly is to create a plan and stick to it. Be sure to keep your utilization rates lower than 25% on your cards and do your very best to pay down your balances in full every month.

Investment Plan Documents – Do you keep copies of all of your investment plan reports, prospectuses, and authorization forms? You should. Do you review your retirement documents on a regular basis? You must! The only way to know how your accounts are performing is to read the reports. Compare the current quarter to the previous quarter and the previous year. Ask questions of your CFP™ when they arise. Don't be shy! It's your money! You have a right and a responsibility to monitor your portfolio. Don't leave it up to anyone else. Be that second set of eyes!

Milestones/Rewards – The great thing about planning proactively is that it allows you to build in rewards for yourself. When you reach a particular milestone, go ahead celebrate a little! You've earned it! Remember, your celebration shouldn't break the bank or interfere with any of the goals that you've set, but when you've worked hard and accomplished what you set out to do, do something to enjoy it.

The best way to do this and not fall into old habits is to include a milestone gift line item in your budget. Small savings towards rewarding yourself helps you feel good about what you've accomplished and helps you stick to your plan!

It's important to control your impulses when it comes to making money decisions. Proactive Planning helps you do this. Consider using the Rule of 72 when it comes to making money decisions. The Rule of 72 simply means that you select a single transaction spending limit, perhaps $100, and that you commit to delaying any single purchase that exceeds this amount for three days.

For many people, impulse buying is dangerous. Impulses exist deep within our subconscious minds and that makes them difficult to control. Whether it's the sweater that's seemingly calling your name, the new phone that performs 25% faster than the one you currently own, or even the pair of Jimmy Choo's that you found on eBay for 30% off the original price. If it's not in the budget it's an impulse purchase. Putting the Rule of 72 into practice helps you control the most dangerous and expensive impulse purchases. Go ahead. Pick a number. I suggest starting somewhere around $50. Any discretionary purchases above $50 will require a three-day waiting period. Try it. See if after 72 hours the urge to buy is still as strong as it was three days ago!

One Final Note on Proactive Planning – I teach my clients an easy acronym to help them incorporate proactive planning into their lifestyles. I teach them that proactive planning gives you **P.O.W.E.R.**

POWER stands for:

P – Pinpoint your current financial status

O – Outline your financial goals

W – Weigh the alternatives

E – Execute your plan

R – Review and Revise as needed

POWER to control your money today; POWER to grow your money for tomorrow; and POWER to take responsibility for your financial future!

CHAPTER FIVE

COMMIT TO TAKING ACTION

Chapter 5

Commit to Taking Action

One day when my youngest son, Tyler, was in the 4th grade, I received a frantic call from him. He was sitting in the principal's office and was pretty upset about an incident that happened while he was in class. Through tears, he told me that his teacher had aggressively pushed him several times. He said he was ok, but wanted me to come pick him up.

Without hesitation, I grabbed my purse and my car keys and made a bee-line to his school. During the 14 minute drive, I could literally feel my blood boiling as my incredulity turned to anger and then rage. By the time I arrived at the school, I was in full mama-bear mode ready to go to battle for her cub!

During the time it took me to get to the school, Tyler must have thought about what might happen when I arrived (he knew I had a very short fuse when it came to my children). I'm sure he realized that it might be a good idea to warn someone of the Category 5 hurricane on her way to the school and who would likely blow the doors off the hinges! I'm not sure if he was feeling bolstered by this backup force coming or if he was truly worried for their well-being. Regardless of his motives, he made enough of an impact on the office staff that someone was standing at the front door waiting for me as I pulled into the parking lot.

Her name was Ms. Lee and she was the school's secretary. Her prepared message was "Mrs. Stephenson, the principal asked me to meet you and escort you into the private conference room." Can you believe this? They knew the exact strategy necessary to take the wind out of my sails and diffuse the situation by immediately escorting me to an area away from other students, teachers and visitors.

Mothers are naturally protective of their offspring. We want the best for them. We want to ensure their safety and happiness. We do everything in our power to provide for our kids. Many of us would be willing to die to keep our kids safe. Those were the thoughts going through my mind as I sped toward the school that day. My son called and I took action!

Taking action is defined as doing what needs to be done when it needs to be done in response to the situation. Can you imagine if we took action when it comes to our finances like we do when it comes to our children or our other loved ones? Can you see the possibilities? Imagine yourself a year from now, after having taken every financial action necessary to get your life on track? Are you smiling? How do you feel? You can make this feeling a reality starting right now. Go take some action.

Why We Stay Stuck In a Financial Rut

When a woman experiences a trauma such as divorce, death of a spouse, or some other disaster in her life, she will experience a myriad of emotions and go through several stages of adjustment. Often, the stress of the trauma is so strong she can do little more than function at the most basic level. Other times, she might find herself focused on other people who are in the situation with her such as her children. Also, she might react by going into survival mode. What happens during survival is this: if the immediate challenge or issue doesn't involve a life or death decision, she simply can't or won't deal with it right then. Other reasons we might find ourselves in a financial rut during the aftermath of trauma include avoidance, resignation, shock or fear of failure.

We avoid dealing with our finances during trauma because we don't want to be any more uncomfortable than we already are. We're too busy dealing with the stress of the trauma. We feel as if adding even one more brick to the load that we're carrying will make it all come crumbling down. We avoid taking action on our finances during this time because we don't really want to deal with our own feelings or thoughts.

We don't want to face the reality of our situation, and sometimes we believe that in order to control or hide our feelings, we have to avoid the triggers that cause them to surface. These feelings can range from hurt, anger, dismay, fear, depression or betrayal to unworthiness, shame, guilt, or sorrow. The truth is avoiding these thoughts and feelings won't make them go away. They will eventually bubble up to the surface. When it comes to your finances, taking action can help counteract some of the negative feelings with positive ones like courage, pride, forgiveness, gratitude and fortitude!

Another reason we stay stuck in a financial rut is because we resign ourselves to the situation. Basically, we give up or we give in. Instead of deciding to take action and move forward, we would rather take no action and wallow in our current state. This can often lead to depression and anxiety. If we sit around telling ourselves that our situation will never improve, that we're not meant to be happy, healthy or wealthy, or that things will never go our way – then they won't. Change begins in the mind. Your mindset is the key to winning this battle. Start there.

After a traumatic experience, you might experience total body shock. When we go into shock, our organs go into survival mode. It's our body's way of protecting itself from further damage. During an actual episode where we experience shock, our organs aren't getting enough blood or oxygen and so things slow down. We may experience low blood pressure and dizziness. Our temperature drops. We get cold and clammy hands. Our brains don't function as well.

Despite the difficulty in dealing with financial issues in the aftermath of a tragedy, you can't ignore the paperwork forever. Your mail is going to pile up. You'll miss important correspondence like bills and past due or renewal notices. If you're not extremely vigilant in the early days after a crisis, you'll probably find it more difficult to get back into the swing of things after a few weeks or months.

It's hard to recognize for yourself when you're exhibiting signs of shock. This is when you really need a friend. A trusted family member or close girlfriend is a must have during times like this. You must stay connected with those who love you most. You will need help and there is no shame in that. Don't be afraid to seek out help and support.

Finally, we often stay where we are because we're afraid we will fail, we won't get it right or we won't finish what we start. The truth is any of those things might happen or they all might happen. However, they will all definitely happen if you never try, start, move forward and take some sort of action.

Shift into Action

The first step to moving out of your financial rut is probably the hardest. When an object is at rest, it actually takes more energy to begin a motion than it does to maintain the motion. The same holds true with you when you're stuck in a rut. The very first step will probably be the most difficult to take. However, it's the most important step to take because without it, you can never build enough momentum to move further along the path to your goals and eventually achieve them. So, let's deal with taking the first step, shall we.

Procrastination is a time killer and a beast of a soul sucker. You have to eliminate procrastination from your life no matter how comforting it feels. Procrastination is avoidance in its most basic form. Instead of doing the uncomfortable, we instead choose what we believe is more comfortable when we procrastinate. The reality is that procrastination not only delays the inevitable, it can also make it worse.

Procrastination often brings with it panic and fear because when we put off something important for too long or even worse, until it's too late, we find ourselves out of options. We feel worse for simply not doing it when there was enough time to get it done.

When it comes to dealing with tough financial issues, it's easy to become overwhelmed with the thought of how long it might take or how difficult it might be or even how having to call creditors to ask for more time to pay makes you feel ashamed. You can't let procrastination take your power.

To break out of procrastination and shift into action follow the following guidelines to start to conquer your financial demons:

Don't try to do it all at once. Break huge tasks down into workable chunks. Remember, you didn't create this financial crisis overnight and you won't slay this dragon overnight either.

Consider working in another environment. Sometimes changing your surroundings helps you stay on task and finish what you've started. Move to a different room. Go to the library or the coffee shop.

Give yourself a deadline. When I'm working under a deadline, I'm much more productive. If you find it tough to stick to your self-imposed deadlines, try giving yourself a small reward when you meet your goal within the timeframe you planned. The thought of a spa day or day trip to the beach works like a charm for me.

Eliminate distractions. Turn off the TV. Silence your cell phone or other mobile devices until you need them to make a call or to gather research. Make sure the kids are bathed, fed, and focused on things that keep their attention long enough for you to finish this project.

Find an accountability partner. Did you know that sharing your goal with another person has a psychological effect on you? Make sure it's someone who will expect you to keep your word and who will hold your feet to the fire if you try to skirt your commitments.

Keep it simple. Don't over complicate it. You don't need a fancy spreadsheet to figure out your finances. A simple pad and pencil will do. If you feel like getting fancy, use colored gel pens or highlighters to spruce up your handwritten budget if you want, but don't make it any harder than it needs to be.

Just do it! Ok, this last one is probably the hardest to read, but sometimes we just have to put on our big girl panties, push our shoulders back, stick our chests out and bite the damn bullet. Let's just get it done and celebrate our successes when we're finished, ok?

Bite the Bullet – The Next 90 Days

I really want to help you take steps toward getting your financial life back together. I'm sure you're ready to take control back or at the very least are thinking about it, otherwise you probably wouldn't be this far into this book. Taking actions is tough and can be a little scary, but having a plan helps. I believe that you can do it.

To help you get started I'm sharing my super-simple 12-week Money Makeover Blueprint with you. Each week is a different action item and I've purposely kept them simple and easy to do. Meticulously follow the plan and after 12-weeks, take notice of your progress. Connect with me on social media (you can find out how in the resources section at the end of the book) or send me an e-mail to share your results. I can't wait to hear how well you've done and how much you accomplish in 12 short weeks. I highlight my readers' successes, and you never know yours might be chosen as one of our Money MOJO Success Features!

The 90 Day/12 Week Plan

Week 1 – Clean out your purse, laptop bag, backpack and anything else you carry around on a daily basis. Clear all the clutter, old receipts, junk mail, old candy wrappers, and anything else untidy. Commit to doing this on the same day, each week for the next 12 weeks.

Week 2 – Organize your household bills and income documents into a filing system. You can use a manual or a digital system. It's up to you. Categorize your bills by utilities, credit cards, mortgage/rent, tuition, medical/dental, charitable giving, etc. Make a folder for each category. Create a "Paid" file to put all of your paid bills into. Organize your paycheck or direct deposit stubs by date and place into a single folder.

Week 3 – Go through your bills and take notice of their status. Catch them all up if necessary. If you can't catch everything at once, create a plan to get caught up over the next few weeks or months. Write your plan down on paper.

Week 4 – Create a budget. I know this isn't fun, but it doesn't have to be hard. Start with a single sheet of paper. Draw a vertical line down the middle. On the left side, write "Income" at the top. On the right side, write "Expenses" at the top. Now list all your monthly income sources on the left and all of your monthly bills on the right. Add them up at the bottom. Subtract your monthly expenses from your monthly income. The answer is your discretionary income. Determine how much of your discretionary income is for groceries, gasoline, household necessities and savings. Subtract these items out next. With the balance that's left over allocate that amount to things like clothing, entertainment and personal expenses like manicures and self-care items. If you run out of money before you account for everything you have two choices – reduce your expenses or increase your income. It's that simple.

Week 5 – Pull your credit report. Visit www.annualcreditreport.com and request copies of each of your credit reports. Read them. Highlight any items that are incorrect or unfamiliar to you.

Week 6 – Dispute incorrect items on your credit reports. Using the links you will find on the websites for each credit bureau, dispute all of the items that are incorrect on your credit report. Keep copies of everything you do. Mark the date on the calendar that you report the information as bad.

Week 7 – Start a savings account. My preference is that you do this through one of the online banks that are available. Two examples of online banks are Ally Bank and Synchrony Bank. You can easily find each by performing a quick Google search. They make it very easy for you to set up a savings account with automated, recurring transfers from your primary bank account. Another option is to visit your payroll department and split your direct deposit into two separate accounts. Simply have the amount that you set aside for savings come directly out of your paycheck and sent to the new account that you've set up.

Week 8 – Check your federal and state withholdings. Are you loaning the government more money than you should each payday? If you're used to getting a big refund at tax time, consider changing your withholdings so you bring that money home each payday. Put it to good use by adding that amount directly to your savings each week.

Week 9 – Protect your assets. Check your insurance policies. Ensure that you have sufficient coverage on your homeowner's, renter's, auto and life policies. Check your medical/dental coverage to ensure that you are using all the benefits you're entitled to. If you are not visiting the doctor or dentist regularly and are healthy enough, but are paying for a policy that has a high premium because it's for people who go the doctor a lot, consider changing your plan type during the next open enrollment.

Week 10 – Check your credit status. Remember the disputes you submitted during Week 6? It's time to go back and check the status of each of them. If the credit bureaus have been unable to verify the debt, they must remove the inaccuracy from your report. Follow up to ensure this is completed.

Week 11 – Review your retirement plan allocations. If you participate in a 401k or a 403b at work, review your quarterly statements. Develop a good understanding of how your portfolio is performing. Contact the administrator if you have any questions. Find out from your HR department when you are allowed to make changes to your contributions and allocations. If you have an IRA, familiarize yourself with the statements for these accounts as well.

Week 12 – Review the past 11 weeks and plan for the next cycle. Take note of what worked well. Did you have inaccurate items fall off your credit report? Did you stick to your budget? Where can you make adjustments? Plan the 12 week cycle out and repeat the process. Build onto the last cycle by repeating or re-working each step. If you completely fix an issue, consider going deeper on another task or breaking it up into two parts for the next cycle. Continue to rinse and repeat every 12 weeks.

One of the biggest deterrents to people taking control of their financial situation is the belief that the problem is too big to be solved. That's not true. Any problem or challenge can be overcome. Breaking it down into manageable bite-sized chunks will help you overcome your financial struggle. You just need a solid plan, good guidance, and the guts to take action.

Taking action is one of the most important commitments you can make to yourself during this process. Yes, each commitment is important, but this one is right up there at the top of the list. You can't just talk about what you want to do and not move. You cannot expect to complain about it and have the problems miraculously disappear. You have to take action. The sooner you put the 12-week plan into place, the sooner you will start to see a light at the end of your money tunnel.

Remember, action breeds momentum. Momentum breeds success. You can be successful at this personal finance thing. I know you can. Commit to getting unstuck. Commit to moving out of your comfort zone. Commit to stop procrastinating. Commit to take action and do something about it starting today!

CHAPTER SIX

COMMIT TO PUTTING YOURSELF FIRST

Chapter 6

Commit to Putting Yourself First

After my divorce, I became the sole provider for two growing boys. They were always hungry, always in need of a bigger pair of shoes, and seemed to need money for something at school at least every other day. To top that off, my youngest son was a member of the marching band at his high school. In our state, there's very little, if any, funding for arts programs at the high school level. This means unless your child is on the basketball, football, or baseball team, you are expected to foot the bill for him to participate in extracurricular activities.

Each year, the band director along with the band's board would calculate the annual band budget. The total budgeted amount was then divided by the number of students in the band that year. This individual amount was called your "fair-share." Each year, our fair-share averaged between $450 and $550 dollars. Fair-share didn't include the uniform fee, (despite uniforms being passed down year to year by the way), marching shoes, transportation costs to the multiple out-of-town competitions or the cost of instruments.

Do you have any idea what a new 'amateur' trumpet costs? As a reward for his hard work, each time your budding musician gets better, you get the honor of upgrading to the next level instrument so he can continue to mature in his musical skill! Ok, yes, I'm being a bit sarcastic, but it's true. We started with a used instrument in the 6th grade and have fully progressed to professional level trumpet in college!

My oldest started college the year after the divorce, and as the responsible parent, I carried the weight of tuition, room & board, books and monthly spending money squarely on my shoulders. It was important to me that my kids had the full college "experience" and I did what I could to make sure that all their needs were met. I regularly cut back on necessities and self-care for myself to ensure they would not have to feel the brunt of my financial burden.

I have really great kids and they are very responsible, but they love nice things and inherited the gadget junkie gene from me! They knew that it was a financial struggle to get them through high school and college. They knew without me ever having to say the words out loud. Despite the pressure I put on them to "tell me about everything," they would try to figure things out on their own before calling home or they would go without a book for a class or something of the like. They did all of this to try to help me save money. It was a stressful time for them and for me. We all thought we were "helping" each other when in reality we should have been more open to discussing the situation and creating solutions together. They were old enough. They were educated. They were emotionally mature, but for some reason we each felt it necessary to deal with the financial stress privately.

I'm sharing these stories with you because as a dedicated mother I know how hard it is to put ourselves first when necessary. I'm not advocating being selfish, shirking your parental responsibilities or expecting your children to buy their own groceries when they're still teenagers. What I am suggesting is the belief that in order to be a "good" mother, we have to neglect ourselves is false.

Why Put Yourself First?

You are your best and brightest asset. Let me say that again a little differently – YOU are your most valuable possession. It's not your home; it isn't your vehicle; it's not the jewelry you own, and it isn't your kids. Taking care of yourself is of the utmost importance! Without you, nothing that you have or created would exist. I believe in the Highest Power, but even in His most infinite wisdom, He used you through which to create everything that you've been a part of. Do you get that? Do you understand that you're a vital part of God's plan for your life and the existence of everything you've touched in this world?

It may be a bit cliché, but there really is a reason that airlines advise in the case of an emergency you to put on your oxygen mask first. The reason is because if you put their mask on first, you run the risk of running out of oxygen before you can get theirs on completely and therefore you both suffer. When you take care of your immediate needs first, you have a better chance at saving both of your lives. When you take care of yourself, you're better equipped to take care of others.

Let's talk about what putting yourself first is and what it isn't.

Putting yourself first means loving yourself enough to know what you need and when you need it. For my entire marriage, I put everyone in my family's needs before my own. I thought that I was doing what I was supposed to be doing as a wife and mother. In doing so, I took notice of their needs and missed out on my own. As a result, I was over stressed, overweight, overworked, and before long, I crashed.

Putting yourself first isn't selfish. It's actually a good thing because when you put yourself first, *everything* else in your life benefits. When you've been through a traumatic experience, it's even more important to take the time you need to heal, bounce back (and yes, you will bounce back), and restore yourself.

What Happens When You Neglect Yourself

There are numerous negatives outcomes when you neglect your own needs and constantly put the needs of others before your own.

It's harder to make tough decisions. The stress that accompanies self-neglect takes a toll on our mental state. When we neglect to pay attention to our own needs, over time this stress builds up and it becomes more difficult to make tough decisions. Under stress, we don't have mental clarity. We simply don't have the energy necessary to think a problem through and come up with a viable solution and then act on that solution.

When you aren't taking care of your personal needs, it's easy for a small financial hiccup to become a financial crisis. Because we struggle to think clearly, we delay or ignore the problem. We think by ignoring our financial problems, they will just disappear. Nothing can be further from the truth. The issue isn't going anywhere on its own. So take care of yourself. Do what's necessary to maintain your equilibrium and mental clarity so you can deal with your financial issues before they reach crisis proportions.

We lose sleep. When we worry, we wreak havoc on our systems. This causes us to lose sleep due to insomnia or simply not sleeping deeply enough to get all of its benefits. The cycle is vicious, because the less sleep you get, the more difficult it is to think clearly. The deeper you get into your financial crisis, the less sleep you get. It's a catch 22 situation.

So, what can you do to remedy the situation? My #1 piece of advice is to be intentional about getting the rest you need and deserve. The recommendation is to shut down all electronic devices at least an hour before bedtime. If you must, take power naps to help you get in the sleep-hours your body craves. Close all the blinds, draw the curtains and use a sleep machine that produces ambient noise or music to help you relax. I use an essential oil diffuser with my favorite relaxation/sleep blend to help me calm down after a long day and so I can decompress enough to let the worries of the day dissipate as I drift off into a good night's sleep.

We mismanage our emotions. Have you ever noticed how easily you become irritated when you're tired? Do you break out crying over things that later seem trivial? Have you wondered why you might be experiencing mood swings? When we neglect ourselves, it becomes more difficult to manage our emotions. We aren't saying "Yes" to ourselves often enough. We're not prioritizing our own needs or are completely neglecting our needs for the sake of others, often to our own detriment.

We make poor food choices and have poor exercise habits. The proper diet and exercise are both vital to helping us maintain good health. I often hear excuses, and sometimes even make them myself, as to why it's too hard or too inconvenient to work out or to eat right.

Let me share an example with you. For years, I struggled to get enough sleep. I'm the type of person who needs her eight hours every night. If I don't, I'm cranky, unfocused, and lethargic the next day. Instead of honoring my internal body clock, I frequently went to bed after midnight making it really tough to wake up on time. Each morning, I'd rush into the shower, get dressed and run out of the door to make it to the office on time. I never had time for a decent breakfast, so I would make a quick pit stop at McDonald's or Dunkin Donuts on my way to work.

For lunch, I always opted for comfort food laced with carbs and sugar. I worked long hours, so dinner was usually something I picked up on the way home from the office. Can you imagine the toll that eating like this for years has taken on my body? I continue to suffer the effects of my poor eating habits to this very day. Yes, I can boldly share with you that it will take a lot of years to counteract the poor choices I made. I share this with you because I believe that transparency is the key to connection.

Divorce, death, and other disasters are not only devastating to our financial lives; they wreak havoc in other areas of our lives as well. I believe that both overcoming these tragedies and turning them into triumphs require a holistic approach. This is the reason I wanted my first book about money to focus on helping you understand the underlying commitments you must first make to yourself if you expect to make a significant and permanent change in your money situation.

Our relationships suffer. Strong relationships start with healthy, whole individuals. To be the healthiest version of yourself, you have to spend time cultivating your own set of values and standards. The highest values and standards come only from knowing yourself well enough to consider, test, reject and accept the beliefs and values that resonate with you. To truly know ourselves, we have to pay attention to our personal needs.

Paying attention to our personal needs cultivates a level of self-trust that no amount of manipulation can curtail. When you fully understand and completely trust yourself, you make more thoughtful decisions about things and issues that impact you. This self-trust happens as a result of seeing yourself through challenging situations and being mindful of both your actions during the incident and your reaction to the steps you took or didn't take and the feelings that come along with those steps.

Knowing and trusting ourselves saves energy. I used to believe that it was easier to just give in if my ex-husband and I had a disagreement. I quickly learned that it's easiest only at the moment of resignation. So often, I lived with self-doubt, anger, and resentment after giving in to his needs without considering my own. Living with those emotions was exhausting. It completely drains your energy and when my energy levels are low, I'm very easily irritated. Being irritated makes it much more difficult to have a rational conversation which leads to communication breakdowns in your relationships. When these breakdowns happen too frequently or last too long, the relationship suffers and sometimes reach the point of disintegration.

What does Self-Care have to do with Money?

I mentioned it earlier and I'll say it again. Self-Care is not about being selfish. It's about knowing yourself well enough to fully embrace who you are and the values and beliefs that you hold dear. Oftentimes when we're married, we lose practice or even completely forget how to make independent financial decisions. We become accustomed to getting advice and or the opinions of someone else; it can be hard to choose what we want to do with our own money.

Another challenge that women face when it comes to making independent financial decisions is fear. According to a *Working Woman* magazine survey, half of its readers worry about becoming financially destitute in their older years. It's no wonder we find ourselves still believing that it's a man's job to take care of the woman and more often than not, end up relying on our ex-spouse's for alimony & child support to help make ends meet. If you fail to protect your own financial needs and learn to handle your own finances before and during your marriage, it's extremely difficult to change your money mindset after the union has dissolved.

If you're single and have never been married before or if you're divorced or widowed and want to remarry, please take my next bit of advice to heart. Never neglect your own financial needs for the needs of the marriage or for the needs of your spouse. While I support joint accounts, be sure that you are donning your own financial mask as well. Insist that you play an integral role in the household finances. Keep some money in an account all your own. Doing so in no way implies that you don't believe in your marriage. It means that you're financially savvy enough to maintain some protection for yourself in the case of an emergency.

If you're dealing with the after effects of a divorce, remember that you have to be your biggest protector during this time. It's not up to your lawyer, the judge, your ex's conscious or anyone or anything else to look out for you! Fight for your financial life! Ask questions. Do your research. Find a great financial adviser outside of your legal advisers. Be sure to gather the information that you need to make wise decisions about your financial future.

If you're dealing with the loss of your spouse due to death and you receive proceeds from a retirement plan or an insurance policy, ensure that your financial needs are covered before offering assistance to adult offspring. It's perfectly acceptable for you to ensure that your financial needs are met first. Don't allow yourself to be bullied or cajoled into giving away money if it will hurt you financially.

If you're taking care of children after divorce, remember it's ok to say "No" to their wants sometimes. Often after a divorce, we try to make up for the pain our children are feeling by over indulging them with material things and gifts. The truth is those material things won't take the pain away. It's better to deal with the pain head on by talking, going to therapy, or family counseling than to by covering up the pain with material things.

Be Fearless and Have Fun

One final note about self-care after divorce, death or trauma:

There is no better time to take life by the balls and have a fun with it! Living your life as an unmarried woman can be a lonely existence if you let it. Don't.

Don't let anger, loneliness and fear stop you from living your life. Pull out your bucket list and start crossing items off as you experience them. If you don't have a bucket list, start one! If you've always wanted to go skydiving, take lessons and do it! If you've dreamed of visiting every state in the country, do it! If you want to go back to school, write a book, sing with a choir, visit a volcano or an ashram, or hike the Himalayas, go for it! Have some fun! You've earned it!

Remember this, while it's fun to do things with a friend, consider knocking some of the items off your bucket list alone. Commit to experiencing life through your own lens. You'll be amazed at what you might learn about yourself in the process!

CHAPTER SEVEN

COMMIT TO PRACTICING GRATITUDE

Chapter 7

Commit to Practicing Gratitude

"A house is not a home, when the two of us are far apart and one of us has a broken heart." ~ Burt Bacharach

A House Is Not a Home

During the fall of 2006, my now ex-husband came home in a really bad mood. I didn't understand why he was angry and it took him a few days to tell me what was really going on. When he finally told me, I learned that he had a disagreement with our landlord. That day, he decided that we were moving and not only were we moving, we were going to buy a house. He was adamant that he wouldn't pay anymore rent to this guy.

By 2006, we had been together for 16 years and had two children. We were living in North Carolina after having moved up and down the east coast every two to three years. In sixteen years, we always rented because we never stayed in a place long enough to put down real roots. When we moved to North Carolina in 2004, we didn't discuss any plans on the amount of time we planned to stay in the area. We also never discussed making the state our permanent home. I was shocked to find out he'd decided to buy a home.

I was shocked for a few reasons. First, buying a house wasn't on my radar screen. We didn't have any money saved. Our credit was pretty bad due to the bankruptcy we'd filed back in 1999. Second, we had no idea where and how to find a realtor, a mortgage broker, or figure out how to pay for a house. Third, he didn't ask my feelings about it at all. He simply made the decision and expected me to live with it.

Fast forward thirty days and a realtor whom we met briefly told us about a subdivision close to our current rental. She said they had two more houses left before they would be completely sold out. We drove over the next day to take a look at the houses. The first house was too small and had less than seven feet of backyard space. We drove to the second house. I got out of the car, looked around back, and walked into the house. My very first reaction to the house was, 'I hated it!'

It had a strange layout. The flooring had been selected. They chose carpet, but I preferred hardwoods. Instead of stainless steel appliances, the builder had already installed builder grade black products. I was promptly told the house was being sold as is and there were no opportunities to make any changes. The next day we heard from the mortgage company.

We were given instructions on what items to fix on our credit report. When we spoke with them, they asked us for the amount of the house we wanted to buy. We'd just seen the house the day before and despite having only seen three houses, we used the details on that particular house to try to get an approval for the mortgage.

Eight weeks later, we moved into our new house and reality began to settle in. Within a few short days, buyer's remorse crept in. I realized that despite all of our bedrooms being on the 2nd floor, the laundry room was downstairs. The first time I had to carry six dirty loads of laundry downstairs only to have to carry them back after they were washed, dried and folded; I realized this wasn't a good setup.

We also realized that our driveway wasn't large enough for all of our vehicles. My oldest son had his license and his own car, so we had three vehicles. Our homeowner's association rules didn't allow on-street parking, so we had a problem. Since my house was the last one built in the subdivision, our lot inherited the street signs, light poles, cable boxes and electrical transformers in our front yard. Imagine sitting at my dining room table and instead of seeing a sea of beautiful green grass, I saw steel posts and massive metal containers that housed the units for everyone who lived on my side of the street. I watched a regular flow of technicians and meter readers walk through my front yard on a daily basis. What had I done? What had I just signed up for?

In the beginning, I hated my house. It felt as if I had settled because my ex-husband's machismo forced him into making a rash decision. The house also held some very bad memories for me since within a year of purchasing it, my marriage disintegrated. I felt stuck and I blamed the purchase of the house for many of my problems. I vowed that I would sell the house the year after my youngest son graduated from high school.

And then something happened. I spent an entire weekend alone in my house. It was September, 2015 and Tyler, my youngest, was tucked safely into the dorm. My oldest son had moved to Florida to begin his life as a personal trainer and fitness instructor. It was just me. As I sat in the quiet, looking at the walls, I began to weep. I was overcome with emotion. I realized that in some weird way, this house was the best thing that could have happened to me and for me. I realized that this house was more than a house, it was a home.

In the years after my divorce, my sons and I became very close. We reformed our family. We laughed. We enjoyed holidays and hosted friends and family in that house. We had pizza and game nights. We celebrated milestones like proms, homecomings and graduations. We endured some of the most difficult times we'd ever faced together in that house. We grew up together in that house.

In that very moment, sitting on my couch, I fell in love with my home. My house became more than just a house. It became my home. Until that moment, I wasn't grateful for the gift that I'd been given. Heck, I didn't even recognize it as a gift! However, at that exact moment, I was thankful that God had sent me this blessing in disguise. I was grateful that I was finally able to see it for what it really was. I even felt a sense of gratitude to my ex-husband for being the catalyst to all of the change that had taken place over the past few years. I realized that had it not been for that impulsivity, we might still be renting a small apartment. I was grateful for every laugh, argument, tear, celebration and victory that occurred while I lived in this house.

In the years since my divorce, my ex-husband and I have entered litigation regarding my home twice. Each time, the judge ruled in my favor and I still live in the home that I once saw only as a temporary. The home has become my sanctuary. It is my place of peace and refuge. It's been 10 years since we bought the house. I initially only expected to live there for a short time, but I'm grateful for the mortgage crisis of 2008, the litigation, the busted air conditioning unit, and even strange layout with the laundry room on the first floor away from the bedrooms. I've come to love my home and I do laundry frequently enough now (every 3 days), so I don't have to carry heavy baskets up and down the stairs. I'm even grateful for the exercise that I get when I am climbing those stairs!

What is Gratitude?

The Oxford Pocket Dictionary defines gratitude as the, "quality of being thankful, readiness to show appreciation for and to return kindness."

Merriam-Webster's definition is a bit more simplified. Gratitude is a feeling of appreciation or thanks.

While gratitude is typically defined in similar ways by most sources, it manifests in a myriad of different ways. Nobody has a patent or trademark on how to exhibit gratitude. Similarly, the way you choose to show gratitude isn't up for debate or discussion. The practice of gratitude is a very personal undertaking and no one but you can judge whether you get it "right" or "wrong." The best anyone can do is communicate how your appreciation impacts him or her, but they can't really say if you're doing it right or not.

I have a friend who often says that when you're not completely satisfied with something that in essence, you're not grateful for it. I disagree. I believe you can be overwhelmingly grateful and still see opportunities for change or wish it were a little different. In my opinion, grateful does not always imply perfection.

Gratitude is your personal expression of thanks or appreciation. It's typically a pleasant feeling that can affect your mood, emotions, and personality. Gratitude can vary in its level of intensity, frequency, breadth and depth. These gratitude dimensions are what I believe makes it difficult for anyone to judge the wholeness or rightness of another person's gratitude practice.

Everyone practices gratitude differently. Whether you feel a slight tinge of thankfulness or are moved to tears, doesn't imply one is more grateful than another. Regardless of the number of people or factors you attribute a positive outcome to, that reason alone does not definitively mean you're more grateful than the person who attributes that same outcome to a single factor.

Gratitude is a positive attribute, but it's also inherently personal.

The Power of Gratitude

The regular practice of gratitude has a tangible impact on our daily lives. Gratitude is a powerful conductor of momentum. I don't want to get to new age in this particular chapter, but momentarily indulge me. Think of gratitude as energy. It's a universal principle that like energy attracts like energy. According to the Law of Attraction, you attract things such as circumstances and situations that are similar with the dominant and habitual thoughts and beliefs into your life. This happens at both a conscious and subconscious level.

This principle is by and far the most powerful trait of strong gratitude practices. Being grateful naturally makes us happier and even more optimistic. When we focus on the positive circumstances and conditions in our lives, we attract other positive circumstances and conditions.

Gratitude is inversely proportional to negativity. It's really difficult to be negative about a situation when your focus is on the positives that could result from it. If you need a mood booster, write down the top five positive attributes of the situation that you're currently facing. Before you think that there are times and situations when you can't find anything positive to think, feel or say, I challenge you to take a deep breath and dig deeper. If you try hard enough, you can find the positive in most situations.

Practicing gratitude helps you deal with problems and develops your problem- solving skills. When we are grateful, we are more open to new and different possibilities, outcomes, and connections. When we're grateful, we are more receptive to life's lessons. Something as simple as the opportunity to learn something new is enough to feel good about and be appreciative for.

How Practicing Gratitude Impacts your Money

Gratitude sends a signal to the Universe. It opens you up to abundance and positivity in your life. Being grateful for the money and resources you currently have, (regardless of how adequate or inadequate it might be), unblocks the path to additional resources to come into your life.

It's important to recognize what abundance looks like so we don't miss the signs as they are presented to us. So often, God sends us blessings, but we don't recognize them as such because they don't match our expectations. Here's an example: You've been unemployed for a year. You've looked everywhere for a job with no real luck. Your unemployment checks ended five months ago and you've just about run through your savings trying to keep the lights on. You run across an ad for a position that would be a few steps backwards from the previous position you held. The job pays $20,000 less than what you made in your former position.

You have the skills for the position. As a matter of fact, you held the same type of role six years ago and excelled. Because you've worked hard to climb the corporate ladder, you worry about submitting for the position because you don't want to feel as if you're going backwards. You talk to a friend about it and she recommends you submit your resume for the position and interview if they call you. Her logic is that at a minimum, it'll be an opportunity to keep your interviewing skills current. You're skeptical at first, but after some thought, you realize that you don't have anything to lose. If you interview and get the job offer, your intention is to accept it and continue to look for something more aligned with your skill-set.

You submit your resume and cover letter and wait to hear back. While you wait, you spend time practicing gratitude each day. It takes three weeks, but you finally receive an invitation to interview. You expect to have a cursory interview with an HR representative, but when you arrive, you're told that you'll be meeting with a panel of interviewers. You find this change a bit unnerving and strange for a position at this level, but since you're already there, you agree to meet with the panel.

During the meeting, you make a strong connection with two of the interviewers. You respond well to their questions which seem more detailed than you would have expected for the position, but because you've been in higher level positions, you're prepared with well thought out and experience-based responses. When the meeting is almost over, you're told that the HR representative will be coming back in to speak with you again shortly. You agree to wait.

When she returns to the meeting room, she closes the door and sits down. She asks you if you have any questions about the position and the company. Most of your questions about the company have already been asked, so you ask a few questions about the role to which you applied. The HR Rep looks at you with a bewildered look and says, "We're not interviewing you for that role. We're interviewing you for the manager role that the other one reports into." She goes on to say, "The person who held the manager's role was promoted last week and his role became available. It's an integral position and we need to fill it quickly. I spoke with the panel and we'd like to make you a conditional offer if you are available to start on Monday." You're also surprised to learn the position pays $2,500 more annually than you made in your previous role.

Let's Chat about Abundance

In the example I just shared with you, the interviewer made a better offer than what was originally expected or hoped for. I believe that the consistent and authentic practice of gratitude creates opportunities to experience abundance in our lives.

What is abundance? It doesn't have to be winning the Powerball Lottery drawing. It's not always a luxury vehicle or vacation. Sometimes it's enough to get you out of a particularly scary situation. Sometimes it's a new job or increased sales in your business. It might be a bonus or a new opportunity to meet the people who can help you achieve your dreams. It might be a judge granting your child support petition including back pay for the months you patiently waited while being grateful for the resources that you did have. It can be all this and more.

Practice Gratitude the Easy Way

Implementing a gratitude practice into your daily life does not have to be some insanely difficult undertaking. It's ok to keep it very simple when exercising gratitude. The key is to be consistent, authentic and committed.

Practicing gratitude is about more than thinking thankful thoughts. Focused attention is important as you build up your gratitude muscle until you develop muscle memory. Eventually, gratitude will be an all-natural, instinctive habit.

Below are five easy ways to incorporate practicing gratitude in your daily life:

Keep a Gratitude Journal – Each night before you go to sleep, take out your journal and make a list of five things that brought you joy that day and for which you are grateful. As you're journaling, include the feelings evoked. Again, it's ok to be grateful for money and the feeling that having enough money creates inside of you.

Use Pictures and Other Reminders – Keeping pictures is a good way to remember what you are grateful for. Writing down the names of your loved ones or experiences that you are grateful for on an index card or sticky note is a great way to highlight your gratitude. Taking the extra step of taping the cards or notes to your bathroom mirror or the refrigerator, serves as an easy way to remind yourself and to regularly practice gratitude. Each time you look at the pictures on your cell phone or see the sticky notes on your mirror, you are reminded of what makes you happy and who you are most grateful for.

Change Your Language – There is a familiar passage in the Bible. It also happens to be one of my favorite. Proverbs 18:21 says, *"Death and life are in the power of the tongue."* Did you know that what you speak has that kind of power?

Practicing gratitude has everything to do with what you say and what you don't say. Remove from your language complaints about your problems. Studies have shown that frequent complaining leads to depression and anxiety. Yes, problems exist for us all, but focusing on them isn't helpful. Instead, focus on attracting the desires of your heart and positive circumstances in your life.

Use Your Planner – Most planners have space to list your to-do items. Many days we only use a portion of the space! In addition to your mirror or refrigerator, your planner is a great place to store little reminders of what you are grateful for.

Each day as you go about your schedule and appointments, it'll be easy to keep track of and add to your list as you are made aware of new people, feelings and experiences to be grateful for.

Volunteer to Help the Less Fortunate – When you place yourself into position to help someone less fortunate, it helps remind you of how blessed you are. Interacting with and experiencing the plight of those facing serious struggles such as homelessness, violence, and hunger creates a sense of compassion that helps you appreciate your own life.

CHAPTER EIGHT

THE BONUS CHAPTER

Chapter 8

The Bonus Chapter

When I came up with the title and the concept for *M.A.D. Money – Money After Death, Divorce, and Disaster*, I never intended it to be a book that blandly regurgitated financial definitions and concepts. There are plenty of books in print that do this well enough already. I didn't want to add another one.

I wanted to connect with women who, like me, have been through traumatic experiences such as losing a spouse to either divorce or death and who are now facing the daunting challenge of taking complete responsibility for her financial well-being. If she's even more similar to me, she's also a woman who is financially responsible for her children. My goal with this book is to help women take a big picture view of their money mindset, motivations, and momentum and be able to make the changes necessary to become stronger when it comes to money. I want to help women understand that money success begins in the mind and with the Seven Commitments that I share with you throughout the book.

However, I realize that you may have picked up this book looking for a more typical approach to financial literacy and a step- by- step, practical plan to help you with your finances. When I finished writing Chapter 7, I decided to add a bonus chapter and share with you the basics of financial literacy. I don't go into explaining each of the steps in detail here, but if enough of my readers connect with me and let me know how M.A.D. Money has helped them and to express interest in reading another book penned by me, I might, just might, consider fleshing the list out in more detail for you. ☺

Here's the 10 Step Plan to help you start your financial journey:

> **Step 1** – Know yourself and your money personality. Fully understand why you treat money the way you do. When we don't understand why we are the way we are, we're doomed to repeat our mistakes over and over again.

> **Step 2** – Develop your financial game plan. Allow for contingencies and substitutions when necessary.

> **Step 3** – Dissolve your debt. Pay off and clean up as much of your current debt as possible. The more debt you have the less money you have for building wealth.

> **Step 4** – Create extra income streams. Use this extra money to build up your savings or for travel.

> **Step 5** – Invest wisely and work with reputable advisers. See Chapter 3 for additional help in this area.

> **Step 6** – Leave a legacy for future generations. Give your children and grandchildren a bit of a head start. Teach them to avoid your mistakes.

> ➢ **Step 7** – Always be learning. Read every financial book and article that you can get your hands on. Ask your trusted advisers to help you understand how you can take what you learn and make it work for you.

> ➢ **Step 8** – Review often. As your money grows never allow yourself to become complacent. Be diligent about regularly reviewing your financial situation.

> ➢ **Step 9** – Be a savvy consumer. You get what you pay for and good quality is always a better choice than cheap poorly manufactured garbage. However, why pay full price if you can use a discount or find it for a lower price someplace else? Need I say more?

> ➢ **Step 10** – Don't forget to reward yourself for your hard work. All fun and no play makes you sad and depressed. If you meet a goal, reward yourself. Enjoy the fruits of all your hard work.

So there you have it. Stay on track to meeting your financial goals and before you know it, the trauma that brought you to this place in life will be little more than a dot in the rear view mirror of your life.

Remember, you can do this! Just follow the guidelines of *M.A.D. Money – Money After Divorce, Death and Disaster* to ensure you have control of your finances instead of the other way around.

Notes:

_____

_____

_____

_____

_____

_____

_____

_____

_____

_____

_____

_____

_____

_____

_____

_____

_____

_____

_____

_____

_____

_____

_____

_____

_____

_____

ABOUT KEMBERLI M. STEPHENSON, MBA

Kemberli Stephenson is the Profit Sherpa. Kemberli is passionate about helping women become financially independent. She's the author of the "M.A.D. Money - Money After Divorce, Death or Disaster' targeted to unmarried women ready to take charge of their financial destiny. Through her 'MAD Money" and 'A Woman & Her Wallet' coaching programs, she empowers women by helping them understand their money mindset and develop a positive relationship with their money. She delivers wealth & money trainings across the country helping thousands of women live richer, fuller lives.

Through her company, AXIS Financial Group, LLC, she helps entrepreneurs achieve strategic, financial, & operational success in their businesses. With over 25 years of corporate finance & 14 years of entrepreneurial experience, Kemberli coaches her primarily female client base to design their dream businesses so they can live a life of Passion, Purpose and Profit. With a focus on her 5 Pillars Business Model, she helps each client reach their Peak Profit Potential by helping her clients streamline business processes while ensuring their financial data is translated into easy to understand and accurate depictions of the business. Kemberli's specialized knowledge of business management and finance/accounting/tax issues, has kept her firm in high demand among entrepreneurs, executives & individuals.

Born and raised in Philadelphia, PA, Kemberli spent several years in the US Navy stationed throughout the country after which she earned a BSBA/Accounting & later her MBA with a concentration in Accounting. In addition to her current coaching practice, she's owned several businesses including a successful accounting & tax firm in Central Florida which she sold when she relocated to North Carolina in 2004.

Kemberli is a dynamic and experienced speaker/trainer and covers topics including Small Business Finance, Entrepreneurship, & Money Management for organizations and associations throughout the US. Kemberli currently lives in the Raleigh, NC area.

RECOMMENDED RESOURCES

Live Workshops & Trainings

Signature Talks

- ➤ M.A.D. Money – Money After Divorce, Death or Disaster™
- ➤ A Woman & Her Wallet™
- ➤ Heels, Hose, & NoDoze™

Workshops

- ➤ Make It Rain – Find Your Money MOJO™
- ➤ Launch then Leap™
- ➤ Crack the Profit Code™

Group Coaching & Self Paced Courses

Personal Finance

A Woman & Her Wallet™ Virtual Training Program

For women who are ready to

- Get to the *real root* of your money *struggles.*
- Learn how to *stop* spinning in *circles* when it comes to your *finances.*
- Create an *ACTION PLAN* that will allow you to *keep* more of the money you *EARN!*
- Get on track (or back on track) and chart the FASTEST course to the absolute *TOP* of your financial potential!

Entrepreneurship

SOAR Entrepreneurial Group Coaching Program™

For emerging entrepreneurs with the desire and drive to create the business of their dreams!

- 9 Weeks of Virtual Group Coaching Sessions
- Understand Your Entrepreneurial Archetype
- Develop Your Transition Plan from Employee to Entrepreneur
- Identify Your Ideal Client Market
- Craft Your Sales & Marketing Plans
- Create VITAL Systems for Your New Business
- Map Out Your Social Media Strategy
- Recorded Sessions

Private Coaching Programs & Sessions

Personal Finance

➢ Budget Breakthrough™ Session

➢ M.A.D. Money Coaching Program™

➢ SLAY Your Student Loan Dragon™ Session

➢ SAVVY Savings™ Session

Entrepreneurship

➢ Jumpstart My Profits™ Entrepreneurial Coaching Program

➢ Breakdown to Breakthrough Session

➢ PUMPS (Power UP My Profits)™ VIP Day/Private Intensive

LET'S STAY CONNECTED.....

I'd absolutely love to hear about the transformations this book creates in your life. Please stay in touch with me. Share your success & triumph stories or your challenges with me by emailing:

hello@kemberlistephenson.com

Also let's stay connected online through these social media platforms:

Facebook: Kemberli Stephenson

Periscope: @ProfitSherpa

Instagram: @ProfitSherpa

Twitter: @ProfitSherpa

Website: www.KemberliStephenson.com

ADDITIONAL RESOURCES

Divorce:
Divorce Care - www.divorcecare.org/
American Bar Association - www.americanbar.org/
National Women's Law Center - www.nwlc.org/
American Association of Matrimonial Lawyers - www.aaml.org/
Association of Family & Concilliation Courts - www.afccnet.org/
Women's Law Center - www.womenslawproject.org/

Death:

Alliance of Hope - www.allianceofhope.org/
American Widow Project (Military Widows) –
www.americanwidowproject.org
Camp Widow – www.campwidow.org
Grief Share – www.griefshare.org

Disaster:

Domestic Violence Hotline - www.thehotline.org/
or Call 1-800-799-SAFE(7233)24/7
Domestic Violence/Financial Abuse Info - purplepurse.com/
Center for Missing/Exploited Children - www.missingkids.com/home
Cancer Patients/Survivors - www.cancer.net/navigating-cancer-care/financial-considerations/financial-resources

Single Parent & Child Support:

National Child Support Enforcement Association - www.ncsea.org/
Parents Without Partners - www.parentswithoutpartners.org/
Single Parent Advocate - www.singleparentadvocate.org/
Single Parent Resource Center - www.singleparentusa.com/

Taxes, Financial Planning & Credit Counseling:

National Foundation for Credit Counseling - www.nfcc.org/
Financial Industry Regulatory Authority – www.finra.org
American Institute of Certified Public Accountants (CPA's) –
www.aicpa.org
National Association of Personal Financial Advisers - www.napfa.org/
National Association of Insurance & Financial Advisers - www.naifa.org/
Internal Revenue Service – www.irs.gov

Starting a Business:

Kemberli Stephenson Entrepreneurship Coach –
www.KemberliStephenson.com
Small Business Association – www.sba.gov
SCORE™ (Free Business Advice) - www.score.org

Retirement:

Women's Institute For A Secure Retirement (WISER) -
www.wiserwomen.org/
AARP – www.aarp.org
Older Women's League - www.owl-national.org/
Social Security Administration – www.ssa.gov

Health Care and Medical:

Health Care Marketplace – www.healthcare.gov
Women & Mental Health - www.nimh.nih.gov/health/topics/women-
and-mental-health/
National Hospice Care - www.nhpco.org/
National Suicide Prevention – www.suicidepreventionhotline.org
or Call 1-800-273-TALK (8255)

www.ingramcontent.com/pod-product-compliance
Lightning Source LLC
Chambersburg PA
CBHW070737220326
41598CB00024BA/3460